KATE O'DELL

CRYSTAL RHYTHMS

Exploring the Energy Potentials of Crystals & Stones

REDFeather

MIND | BODY | SPIRIT

4880 Lower Valley Road, Atglen, PA 19310

This book is dedicated to
the Daughters of Peg, for their innate strength and power
to say what they mean and mean what they say.

Other Schiffer Books on Related Subjects:

Carry Me Crystals—Chakra Clearing & Oracle Card Deck, Joanie Eisinger, Elizabeth Jarvis & Peter Jarvis, ISBN 978-0-7643-5008-5

Type set in Avenir & Chronicle

ISBN: 978-0-7643-5794-7
Printed in India
6 5 4 3

Published by Red Feather Mind, Body, Spirit
An imprint of Schiffer Publishing, Ltd.
4880 Lower Valley Road
Atglen, PA 19310
Phone: (610) 593-1777; Fax: (610) 593-2002
E-mail: Info@schifferbooks.com
Web: www.redfeathermbs.com

For our complete selection of fine books on this and related subjects, please visit our website at www.schifferbooks.com. You may also write for a free catalog.

Schiffer Publishing's titles are available at special discounts for bulk purchases for sales promotions or premiums. Special editions, including personalized covers, corporate imprints, and excerpts, can be created in large quantities for special needs. For more information, contact the publisher.

We are always looking for people to write books on new and related subjects. If you have an idea for a book, please contact us at proposals@schifferbooks.com.

CONTENTS

INTRODUCTION

Many of today's most popular New Age beliefs and practices for living a healthy and balanced life derive from ancient Eastern philosophies. From chakra balancing to yoga, we are witnessing a resurgence of ancient wisdom to address the mental, physical, and spiritual imbalances of our high-stress, technology-driven lives. Among these is renewed interest in the Earth power contained within stones and crystals. For example, ancient Egyptians used stones for protection, health, and adornment, while the ancient Indians saw the energies of gemstones as expressions of the planets and deities. Crystals were, and still are, seen by the people of India as invaluable to redress negative karma as revealed through Vedic astrology. Romans used crystals as protective amulets, as did Greek warriors, who smeared crushed hematite over their bodies for protection before battle. In short, throughout human civilization, people have recognized the inherent powers held within the mineral kingdom.

The use of crystals and stones piqued my curiosity nearly forty years ago, after purchasing my first quartz. I'd read with mounting interest various references to the crystals in my growing collection of New Age books. Over time I developed a rising concern in this subject and found myself researching many of the various claims made about the stones. More recently, I've felt that much of the available information, especially on the web, has been inflated, or at least misconstrued. So many attributes have been linked with every stone that you are led to believe any crystal is a miraculous magical token. It's as if your life will instantly be turned around if you have that special stone in your pocket. There's a stone for every ailment to use as a cure for every disease. Unfortunately, this is an oversimplification that does a great disservice to this alternative healing therapy when the miracle fails to occur. The reality is much more complex.

I've come to believe that the help you receive from working with crystals and stones is an exchange of energy between the crystal and the user. I reached this conclusion based upon my general interest in science and my studies in the metaphysical realm. The most striking concept I have learned is what quantum physics teaches us: All matter in our physical world is simply an expression of energy. Experiments and mathematical computations for the past hundred years have shown physicists that every molecule, every cell, every atom is merely the manifestation of energy. The atom's rate of speed, or frequency, is what creates the physical world we perceive. This means that all plants, animals, minerals, and the Earth itself, spring from their own unique subatomic rhythms of energy. The truth is that matter is an illusion our minds create, and reality is simply a far stranger thing than we think it is. There is a certain plasticity of our world that allows for seemingly miraculous events to occur. This fact is what opens the door to the possibility that metaphysical phenomena can occur.

That is why I believe that the healing and other qualities attributed to crystals and stones can take place.

So, it follows that each individual person's body has its own bioelectrical rhythm. The key, then, is to find a crystal or stone that is in harmony with your own rhythm. Only then can an exchange of energy occur that is beneficial to you. Whether it's to assist your physical body's energetic meridians into returning to a state of balance or to aid you in attracting more-ethereal considerations, crystals and stones can be that catalyst.

Finding the proper stone is a subjective experience. We all emit slightly different energetic frequencies that can show through our personal taste, temperament, and ego. It's this slight variation in frequency that makes all the difference in the world in how you will benefit when using certain crystals and stones. I believe this to be especially true when it comes to helping with healing ourselves. With the right stone, the energy exchanged between it and the user should restore balance along the meridian system and chakras. By restoring normalcy to these energetic fields, it's believed that the manifestation of self-healing can more readily occur.

This book aims to give you some basic information on the chakras and meridian systems, and on choosing the right crystal for your purpose. I have listed eighty of the most popular crystals and stones that I've worked with and sold through my own crystal shop in Gettysburg, Pennsylvania. More than just healing associations, you will find other references, such as how some crystals connect to the devic or fairy realms, as well as suggestions related to their ability to increase your psychic awareness and other non-health-related attributes. My hope is that this book will satisfy your curiosity and assist you in living and benefiting from the use of crystals and stones in your daily life.

Please Note: This book cannot be used as medical advice. As with all alternative methods of healing, you should always seek your doctor's guidance for any disease or illness you are experiencing. The following pages are an attempt at explaining the workings of the healing crystals and stones on a metaphysical level and are not meant to replace any medical advice given from your doctor. The stones are not going to give an instant cure where modern treatments cannot. They are simply meant to use as an adjunct to supplement the spirit of the person with the true hope of bringing about an internal manifestation of self-healing.

CRYSTALS IN YOUR DAILY LIFE

I'm constantly amazed at the diversity of people who come into our shop to buy crystals. So many people have discovered that crystals can improve more than healing in their lives. People purchase crystals and stones for reasons as common as possessing a lucky charm to protecting themselves from unseen ghosts! Indeed, crystals and stones have been used historically to offer a wide range of benefits, from instilling courage in battle to protecting those who carried them. For instance, in times past, bloodstones were used to help staunch the flow of blood from wounds and to rejuvenate the vitality of those in failing health. The purple color of the amethyst was associated with wine and was used to help those who imbibed too much to gain self-control over their addiction. Archeologists believe the ancient Sumerians used different crystals when practicing their magical arts. You can see that crystals and stones have been used since the beginning of recorded time for many things and are once again gaining recognition in the West for their seemingly innate abilities to generally help us in life.

Many of my experiences with crystals and their abilities came to me as the proprietor of The Crystal Wand. For example, a dark-haired young man came in one day asking to see protection stones. After speaking for a few moments on why he was seeking protection, he identified himself as a marine. Apparently, his sister had sent him one while he had been deployed, and he carried it religiously in his pocket. He explained that he had lost it after returning home and now was being deployed for a second tour back to a combat area. He told us that though he couldn't explain it, that rock in his pocket made him feel safe, and he didn't want to go back "over there" without one. That is why he came in, to find another one of those black stones to carry with him. After a brief discussion, we helped him find a black tourmaline that we gave to him as a gift, thanking him for his service.

Last year a young mother came in who had a child diagnosed with attention deficit disorder. The doctors had suggested the usual drug therapy, but she was hesitant to put her son on it. She was searching for something that would help him stay focused in school and stop acting out. After looking over various choices, we picked out a lepidolite and blue lace agate for him to carry in his pocket each day. She said that if it didn't work, she might have to go with the doctor's suggestions, and we agreed. A week later, however, another woman came in looking for something to calm down her daughter. She was referred to us by the first woman whose son had behavioral problems. Apparently, the stones she puts in his pockets every day were helping. However, please realize that what may appear to work for one child will not work for every child. We often suggest stones to help calm children down, but always advise listening to your doctor.

Over the years, many customers have told me how using crystals has helped them. People have found relief from pain or have gotten a good night's rest when keeping stones or crystals on their persons. Teachers come in frequently, referred by other teachers, in search of the stone they need to keep stress levels down or dispel the negative energy they feel from some of their students or coworkers. Nurses, too, come in seeking stones to deflect the oppressive atmosphere surrounding them at work, from difficult patients to overworked staff.

A further example is when one day an elderly gentleman from out of town came in complaining about the arthritis in his hands and wrist. He was attracted to the iridescent sparkle of a labradorite, and though it was not the normally suggested stone for this ailment, he purchased a palm-sized stone. He returned to our shop a few months later to let us know that the labradorite cleared his pain. He said that he carried it around the whole day and went to sleep holding on to it that night. The next morning when he awoke his arthritic pain was gone and had stayed gone! Occasionally, he said, his pain returns, but when it does, he just picks up his stone and carries it around for a while until it goes away. A labradorite might not work for the same condition in another person, but it did the trick for him. I believe this is a clear case of being in harmony with the right stone. This man has his own successful business and was preparing to retire when he experienced this healing. Now that he is retired, he comes to town several times a year with his wife and always stops in to see what new stones we might have.

Personally, I can't type more than two minutes without having a severe aching pain in my wrist that seems to go up my arm. My doctors said it might be carpal tunnel, or it could simply be my arthritis. I knew it wasn't arthritis as the pain I had experienced in my knees and hips was a different kind, so I assumed it was carpal tunnel. I first tried wearing a wrist brace, as the doctors suggested, but to no avail. I then went into the shop and looked around at the stone chip bracelets we carried to see which one might work. I tried a multicolored fluorite and then a purple lepidolite (one of my personal favorite stones), with some relief—but not enough. I then went to the old standby from my grandmother's generation and put on a copper bracelet with magnets attached. That helped some, but still, not enough. I then tried a light-blue amazonite bracelet, figuring the cooling effect of that stone might dampen the inflammatory reaction of my nerves. It was like a miracle. The combination of the magnetic copper bracelet and the amazonite worked like a charm. I could type for hours with no pain. I have been wearing this combination for over three years now whenever I have work to do on my computer. If I do not wear these bracelets, I can type no more than a few minutes without the pain returning. This is yet another example how life can be enhanced by working with crystals and stones.

All these examples show average people who have discovered the beneficial effects of working with crystals and stones. Does it help if you meditate with your crystals? Yes, I believe it does. However, as you can see, they can work for regular people who simply do not think they have the time or the energy to do a healing meditation. If you are focused on what you need and have chosen the right crystal, it will help you achieve what you are seeking.

People from all walks of life, from teens looking to attract romance to seniors wanting to ease their pain, can benefit from working with crystals and stones. All you need to do is find the crystal or stone that harmonizes with you. Hopefully, this book will lead you in the right direction to do just that. In the next few chapters I will give brief explanations on the energetic fields that surround us, and offer samples of different healing techniques. I will guide you through the basic theories related to the color influence of stones and crystals. I have included individual descriptions of eighty of the more popular ones. You will find a usage chart at the end of the book to help you find the crystal or stone you need. Remember, only you can choose the stone that is right for you. Join me now as we enter the realm of possibilities!

AURAS, MERIDIANS, AND CHAKRAS

When learning about crystals and stones, you need a basic understanding of the aura, the meridians, and the chakra system. Most of the information regarding the use of crystals and stones refers to their relationships with these etheric systems and fields. The following are brief interpretations to get you started in understanding the subtle energies that surround you.

Auras

Quite simply, the aura is an emanation of energy that comes from, and envelopes, the physical body. It is believed to reflect our state of health and mind. Some people claim to be able to see and read the auric fields and notice the subtle variations that point to disease or disorders of the person they are reading. By clearing this auric field of negativity and attachments, we can induce a healthier state of being for ourselves. Personally, I tend to think of this auric field as spiritual, a product of the soul. Some believe it is basically an electromagnetic field that the physical body discharges. It surrounds us like a whole-body halo. Others think the colors of your aura can show your emotions as well as the condition of your physical state. If you are angry, red will be seen to flash around you; if you are happy, yellow or bright greens will show themselves in your auric field. There are many books on the subject that try to teach the lay person how to see the aura of others. Be mindful that it takes a lot of practice and faith in yourself to accomplish this feat. One time, while practicing with a friend, I did manage to see a glow appearing around her, though it was hazy and dim. I felt, more than saw, an impression of the color lavender. This attempt was frustrating as I expected to see the colors of the auric field more distinctly. Still, I have met a few people who insist that they can see them clearly and often. I believe them, even though I don't appear to have that special talent, or at least the time and focus to develop this gift. If you wish to cultivate this ability, it helps to spend time in practice with someone who already possesses the faculty. You can also do some research, online or at the library, for hints on how to hone this special skill.

Whether or not you can learn to see or read an aura, I believe in their existence as a bioenergy field that surrounds the body. I think their strength or weakness is a reflection of our physical as well as our emotional and mental health. Therefore, it only makes sense to want to see this field cleansed of any negative attachments and fortified or strengthened to act as a subtle protective force shield that surrounds us. Through meditation with or by carrying the proper crystal or stone, we can achieve this cleansing and fortification on an ethereal level. The ultimate hope is that through this practice we will then feel better and find ourselves living our lives optimally.

Meridians

Thousands of years ago, the ancient Chinese believed that good health came from a balance of chi, or the vital life force that runs throughout the body. They mapped these energetic pathways inside the body that today we call the meridians. It is important to realize that they are lines of energy for the flow of chi, and not something physical inside the body. The ancient Chinese also noted points along these meridians they felt related to the internal organs and other systemic operations of our physical body.

In China, this ancient belief gave way to the art of acupuncture, which was developed to enhance the flow of this chi. It was believed that most diseases or disorders were a result of blockages or disruption in the flow of chi in the body. To restore health to a person, manipulation by use of long, thin needles that were pushed into certain points along the meridian paths would clear the blockage and help a person's body to resume its normal healthy function.

Reflexology is another alternative therapy that was also developed in later years upon the theory of these energy meridians. Both practices are based upon clearing the blockages within this system and allowing the body to heal itself.

In the past, when crystals and stones were used for healing, how they worked was unknown. Now it is believed that they too can influence these ethereal meridians, clearing energy blockages, and promoting the natural free flow of chi. These dynamic meridians run close to, but not exactly in line with, the physical nervous system.

Chakras

The chakras were initially spoken of in the Upanishads, an ancient Hindu text. Here they are explained as wheels or vortexes that draw the spiritual energy from the creative life force into the human body. They were essentially wheels of divine energy found inside the body. They are focused upon in meditation for the purpose of keeping the body healthy and, ultimately, connecting with our divine source to reach enlightenment. Originally, they were meditated on, considered a way of joining the body into a spiritual union with the Supreme Brahman. The ancient Hindus would focus their meditations as they attempted to unleash the base energy at the root chakra, known as the kundalini force. By doing this, they believed this energy would travel up the spine and into the crown chakra, bringing enlightenment and union with the Cosmic Totality.

Over time, these energy centers were seen as doorways to restore healthy functioning in the body. By attuning the spirit with the divine energy of the universe, it is only natural that the physical body would function in an optimal state of being. The use of healing crystals and stones is believed to help open and clear these energy centers, allowing for this form of natural healing to begin.

It is interesting to note that in the original Upanishads, there is no mention of color associations with these energetic wheels or vortices. That came much later and has been most prominent in Western literature, starting around the time of the Theosophical Society. The colors that have been associated with the chakra centers do seem to fit and, for that reason, have been accepted by practitioners of alternative therapies. What follows is a description of each of the main chakras, their association with our body parts, and the colors linked with each one.

1st Chakra—Root

Located at the base of the spine is the site of the kundalini force that's filled with an energetic potential that should only awaken after his or her spirit has been purified through regular meditations. The root chakra is also connected with feelings of security and survival. It's where our sense of stability comes from, as it grounds us to the earth from which our bodies sprang. If it's hard to keep focused on task, you can be helped by clearing and energizing the root chakra. In healing therapies, it is linked with the lower spine, legs, and feet as well as with the adrenal glands. This first energetic wheel is red in color, and so red stones are naturally recommended for use in related healings. It should be noted, however, that black and brown stones are also associated with this chakra as they are grounding, earthy, and stabilizing to the person who carries or wears them.

2nd Chakra—Sacral

Found about two inches below the navel, close to the pelvic area, the second chakra is associated with your sexuality and creativity and has influence over your emotional nature. It is where the emotions that originate from our sexual attractions and rejections come into play. Innate desires and urges spring from here and, when out of balance, can manifest as jealousy and possessiveness.

Meditations focused on the sacral chakra can help us remain calmer in the face of these tempestuous urges and restore balance to our reactions in charged situations. Anger and rage are symptomatic of this energy wheel being out of balance. The sacral chakra is also the center for healing problems that are localized in the sexual organs, kidneys, and lower back and colon. Orange is the color seen to connect with this chakra, and normally orange-tinged stones are suggested for healings in this area of the body.

3rd Chakra—Solar Plexus

Located in the mid-stomach area of the body, this chakra corresponds to your willpower and inner strength. It is where our self-confidence and self-control originate. Focusing on this chakra builds self-esteem and vitality and gives strength to our desires and the ability to manifest what we want in life. When this center is blocked or sluggish, a person may appear cowardly or egotistical. Both are symptoms of the energy in this chakra being out of balance. Its location associates it with physical problems in the region of the stomach, gall bladder, small intestines, and pancreas. Opening and clearing of this center aids the digestive processes and the metabolism, as well as assisting you in losing weight. The color associated with the solar plexus chakra is yellow, and, therefore, yellow crystals and stones are meditated upon or used in conjunction with healing layouts and therapies.

4th Chakra—Heart

This chakra is naturally found near the heart area of the chest. It is linked to the emotional center of our bodies where our feelings of love, compassion, and empathy emanate. This is the center to work on when experiencing feelings of grief or when you are overwhelmed by any emotion that is connected to love or its loss. When you see someone who appears cold hearted or withdrawn, often it is because of blockages in the heart chakra. Cleansing and healings on this energy center aid physical disorders related to the heart, liver, lungs, and circulation. It is also linked with the thymus gland and endocrine system as well as the upper back and tension held in the shoulders. Green is the color linked with the heart chakra, but many have found that the pink stones work just as well, especially with emotional problems linked to love or its loss.

5th Chakra—Throat

Centered in the throat, this chakra focuses on self-expression and speaking your truth. Working on it can help with public speaking, such as delivering a lecture or teaching a class. Clearing this area also benefits sales people and those trying to push through new ideas. Wearing the right crystals and stones can help you with problems related to verbal communication, such as stuttering or other speech impediments. The throat chakra is associated with the lymph glands and is also linked to the thyroid, aiding growth of the physical body. Stimulating this chakra center can help with issues that deal with jaws, teeth, and upper neck, as well as laryngitis, sore throats, and the like. Blue is the color of this energetic wheel in the chakra system, and blue stones are also noted as an aid to inspire creativity in artists and artistic endeavors in all forms.

6th Chakra—Third Eye

The space between the brows is considered the location of the spiritual third eye. By opening and clearing this chakra you can enhance your inner visions, increase your psychic awareness, and open a link to higher-level realms and beings. It's believed that when connecting with these advanced spirits in meditation, you promote the growth of your own spirit, raising it to a state of enlightenment. Most sources link this center to the pineal gland. Wearing the proper crystal, or using it in healing meditations, can clear blockages, release negative attachments, and physically aid disorders of the eyes, ears, nose, as well as headaches and sleep disorders. It can also be useful for issues related to the front of the brain. Indigo and purple are the two main colors linked to this chakra, and purple stones such as amethyst and charoite are frequently recommended for use in this area.

7th Chakra—Crown

The crown chakra is located at the very top of the head and is where the white light of the universe enters the body. This light flows down out of the ether into the crown, traveling throughout all the chakras, giving them the spiritual energy needed to support life. It is the ultimate pathway to the illuminating union with the universe. It also aids communication with angelic and other higher-realm beings. Working on this chakra raises your consciousness and lifts you from the distractions of daily life, allowing you to expand your understanding of the reality of your existence. Clearing and opening this top chakra expands your awareness and brings peace to the soul. Physically, it can be used in healings for brain-related disorders or diseases, mental aberrations, and headaches. White is the color most often associated with this chakra, but violet can work here as well.

Please remember that these are simply the metaphysical traits and qualities ascribed to the chakra centers and their associated physical parts and systems. You should never substitute the use of crystal healing for any medical treatment or medication you are currently taking. We advise everyone to check with their doctors or healthcare professional for medical advice. The use of the healing crystals and stones is strictly something you can do for yourself as an additional alternative therapy to supplement or complement whatever treatment or drugs you are currently taking. Do not substitute one for the other.

FINDING YOUR CRYSTAL

Choosing the crystal that will work for you can be challenging at first. In my shop we recommend that a customer start by walking around the displays and simply pick up one that attracts their attention. We advise holding on to it, closing one's eyes, and taking a deep breath. We ask them to focus for a moment and try to feel the energy of the stone. If it doesn't feel like anything, or they simply do not like the looks of it, then put the stone back and try another. A person must trust their instincts and let their own natural reaction to the stone be their guide. Quite often I see customers drifting back to one of the crystals they had been drawn to earlier but had put back in the display bowl as they continued their search. It seems that most people want to check out all the stones first before making a decision. They seem apprehensive about making that choice. This isn't a life-or-death matter, and it usually doesn't cost more than a dollar or two. Take that leap of faith and choose two or three crystals to work with. In time you will know which one is the correct one for you. And you can always give the stone you decide isn't for you to a friend. It might just be perfect for him or her.

Selecting a stone or crystal is a subjective experience and one that, in time, will become easier to do. Remember, all you are doing is making an intuitive choice instead of a practical one. And once you are comfortable with trusting your instincts, the whole process becomes easier. Just because someone told you that you had to have a green aventurine to heal your broken heart doesn't mean it is the right stone for you. I might advise you to look at and pick up several different stones associated with the heart chakra. They all have similar vibratory rhythms, but one will stand out, draw you in, sing to you, as it were. Go with that stone. It may be a translucent rose quartz, or a striped, deep-green malachite. By checking the chakra chart in this book, you will see that the heart chakra relates to the pink stones as well as the green ones. Your friend may just be a green-stone person, but you could resonate better to the pink-colored crystals. As stated before, it is a subjective experience and one that in time can become second nature to you.

For example, let's say you and your partner have split up, and you bought a rose quartz, slept with it, carried it, and even found time to meditate with it, but still felt depressed over your broken heart. Stop and take a few moments to think about your emotional state and why you are having so much difficulty feeling better. Then, go back and try a different crystal. See what other stones in the heart chakra grouping were calling to you. Or you could try a different approach and simply look for one that will lift your spirits. The yellow, white, clear, and orange stones are good choices for that. Perhaps, using both stones is what your spirit needs to help you feel like your old self again. Some people find solace in a white stone such as scolecite as it helps raise their spiritual level to a higher plane, making angelic connections easier. Perhaps that is what is needed: a good spirit-to-spirit or soul-to-soul talk with your guardian angel to help you get over your loss. There are as many ways the stones can help as there are causes for each problem or disorder.

The crystals and stones help the spirit, the aura, and the soul move closer to a union with the Universal Light, God, Goddess, or whatever you may call your supreme being or ultimate source of life. It is through this connection that a spiritual healing takes place in the auric field or the energetic meridians. From there, the physical form can draw the restorative energy in, allowing your emotions, as well as your physical body, to begin repairs in a perfectly natural way.

You will know when you have chosen the right stone for your purpose when you realize that you are feeling better, whether coming back from an emotional overload or noticing that the pain in your back is dissipating. For those who choose a red or black stone for grounding themselves, when you find that you are more focused on your task and not getting lost in flights of fancy, you will know. If you have been anxious and stressed and started wearing a deep-pink rose quartz or light-blue lace agate pendant and find that you have been walking around calm and serene all day, you will know. And maybe if you have always been a little shy or fearful of others and so started to carry a piece of orange carnelian or a red jasper, then suddenly realize that you are standing up for yourself and walking tall, you will know.

Just remember, the crystals and stones are Nature's way of helping you help yourself by clearing your auric fields and chakras of negative attachments and small tears. When crystals are in sync with the person using them, they help fortify your energetic meridians and open your chakra centers so that the light energy of the universe can freely flow, restoring the physical manifestation that is your body to a more proper way of functioning.

CRYSTAL CLEANSING

The energetic cleansing of your crystals and stones can be accomplished by several methods. I believe that any one of the methods can work, because, ultimately, we are dealing with the clearing of negative energy vibrations, something that is not substantially physical in this realm. Therefore, it follows that the intention of your cleansing is just as important, if not more so, than how you do it. Your own belief system will dictate what works best for you. I believe it is your personal energy acting as the catalyst to clear away the negative energy and recharge the crystals or stones. I say this because the more you read about cleansing procedures, the more methods you will see. Some books or websites will insist on salt water, and others will explain how salt robs the crystals of their luster. Some act as if regular tap water is fine as a bath for the stones, while others will tout the energy of natural rivers and streams. Still others will recommend leaving them outside in the sun or buried in the earth for a day. Therefore, I will list several of the more popular methods, and you can choose which one feels right for you—then use it!

Cleansing the stones is important because they do accumulate negative energy. You will notice them working less effectively, and some people can truly feel the difference when they handle their crystal. It might feel heavier, or somewhat repellent. Remember, the energy of the crystals is essentially the manifestation of their vibratory nature. Their frequencies can entangle with the surrounding negative, as well as positive, vibrations. The energetic power of our minds, acting as a catalyst, cuts through these entanglements and cleans up these vibratory patterns more so than any precise ritual or form used. Cleansing the crystals breaks this mix of energies,

allowing the crystal or stone to return to its natural state. Without this focused intent behind any style of cleansing, the clearing of the stone won't be as real or beneficial. But with intent, I can set a stone in a bowl of salt water, hold my hands over the bowl, and will the negativity away. Or if I am smudging, I only need to believe that smudging will do the trick. And with sunlight, simply believing the natural solar radiation falling upon the surface of the crystal is burning away the negative vibes will work. All of these are good methods— it's simply a question of using your own intuitive choice.

The Water Cleanse

Let's begin with the basic water cleanse. In earlier times, water was used to ritually cleanse or bless more than sacred items. John the Baptist immersed his followers in a river to symbolize their rebirth as a purified soul preparing for the coming of the Messiah. To this day in Christian churches around the world, baptism is performed to clear away original sin or to symbolize the dedication of a person's soul to Jesus. Of course, through the centuries, it has been modified by many sects, from dunking in a river to pouring water or oil over the forehead of an infant. Another example of a water ritual is when Hindus make pilgrimages to the Ganges in India to submerge themselves and bathe in these holy waters. Once again, it is a ceremony to clear them of sins and refresh their spiritual selves. Substitute the term "negative energy" for sin, and you can understand this

practice. This spiritual cleansing started with the running water of rivers, streams, and oceans; however, that is not practical in today's modern world. Most people have access only to water that runs from their taps. Therefore, we work with what we have. With the infusion of your mental energy, you can charge the water that flows over the stone. And that energy is what is going to clear the harmful energies from the stone. The charged water is simply your physical tool for doing so.

Salt water is the preferred method of cleansing by many who believe in the protective powers of salt. Sea salt is the preferred type of salt for this style of cleansing. For this, you merely fill a bowl of water and add about a tablespoon of salt to a small bowl and two or three for a large one. Place your stones or crystals in the water and let sit overnight. Rinse them off with clear water in the morning to remove any traces of salt residue that may dull or mar the surface of the crystal or stone. And remember, some stones and crystals, especially the polished or tumbled variety, will dull in time under a saltwater bath!

The truth is that some stones lose their sheen or other attractive properties when they are either water-cleansed or saltwater-cleansed. Tumbled stones you purchase are polished, and when this polishing has been eroded, they will no longer appear as they initially did. The safest stones for salt or water cleansing tend to be those of the quartz family, agates or jaspers. There are other stones that simply degrade in water, and it's best to clear them with other methods. Some stones or crystals that should NEVER be water-cleansed are all of the selenites, especially desert cactus or cactus rose. Water will degrade these stones as they are ultimately water soluble. They may not fall apart the first time, but it will weaken them and over time they will begin to crumble. These are stones that are normally found in desert regions and simply can't take the action of water on their surfaces. Crystals and other stones that don't do well over time with water cleansing are those that contain copper or iron. Some examples are malachite, pyrite, chrysocolla, and hematite. These stones can be best cleared by setting them among amethyst or hematite crystals or by laying them out in the sun or moonlight. Smudging them with sage or a sage blend is also an appropriate method of cleansing.

Sunlight/Moonlight Cleanse

This method is one that I most often use: sunlight. Set your stones in a sunny window or in your yard in a sunny spot. The energy of the solar rays can clear the negative buildups from your crystals and stones. The only caveat here is that some of the clear-colored crystals, such as amethyst, citrine, and celestite, will see their colors fade when left in the sun too long. This is simply the bleaching action of sunlight on the crystal, and so these stones are best cleared with water, salt water, or smudging. Another method of clearing the more sun-sensitive stones is setting them in a bowl of hematite crystals. They are great energy cleansers and can draw the harmful vibes from the crystals set among them. In turn, then you can clear your hematites in the sun to recharge them and get them ready for the next time you need to use them.

Moonlight is the favored method of other crystal enthusiasts. For this cleansing and recharging, you set your stones out so that the rays of the full moonlight fall on them overnight. This is a good method for the sun-sensitive stones, especially amethyst, and, of course, moonstone and pearls or mother-of-pearl. Some people believe in letting them set out for the entire two-week period of the waning moon to thoroughly clear them. Others prefer to set them out for the two weeks of the waxing moon to recharge them. Personally, I simply keep the stones I am not currently using on the window sill and feel as though this works for me.

Smudging

I also like smudging, a ritual that has been used by Native Americans for clearing, purification, and healing. In the past, the burning of sage or other herbs has been used to keep insects away, as well as to prevent disease from spreading. Modern science has found that the smoke from burning sage does in fact have antibacterial qualities that can cleanse the air. So, it is no wonder that this old custom has found new popularity in our modern world. When used to clear crystals and stones, this method is simple. Take a sage or sage combination smudge stick and light it. Once the flame has died out, you pass the crystal or stone through the smoke while focusing your mind on clearing out the negativity. This technique always felt right to me and is probably the least likely to cause any undue damage, fading, or cracking of the stone itself.

Whether you smudge or use running water, natural water, the ground, or sun or moonlight, just remember: the most important aspect of any cleansing is the intention held within your mind.

Now, a point that everyone does agree on is that you should cleanse any new crystal or stone you buy before you use it. The premise for doing this is because of the variety of people who have handled it. The crystals and stones you purchase have been dug out of mines, then processed and sorted by many different people. Add to that the handling by prior customers and you can see the potential for being contaminated by harmful vibrations. That's the reason you clear the crystals and stones before you program them to work for you.

Programming

Programming is another step in the process of attuning with your crystal or stone. After you have cleansed it, sit down somewhere quiet and relax. Hold it in your hand and think about what you want from it. Are you seeking a healing? Then visualize that healing energy flowing from the stone into your body. Are you seeking prosperity? Then concentrate on the good luck that will come your way in the form of cash in your pocket. Are you using it for courage and strength in times of need? Then focus your thoughts on standing tall and firm in your convictions. Just spend a few minutes bonding with your stone if you

want a more satisfying experience with it. Those of you who are acquainted with meditation will find it easier to spend more time truly connecting with your chosen crystal and may experience more-intense results.

Meditation can be an entire lesson in itself. If this is an area of interest for you, I would suggest taking a course, perhaps at your local Y, watching online lessons or videos, or buying a book on the subject. There are many types of meditation, from transcendental to simple mindfulness. Once again, this is a personal choice, and only you know which method will feel right.

As we end this chapter, an important fact to remember is that crystals and stones are not diamonds! Depending on where each stone is found on the Mohs Hardness Scale, crystals and stones can break, fracture, chip, or denigrate. Hematite comes to mind as one crystal that breaks easily; so can amethyst, citrine, quartz, and, honestly, most others. I have more broken and dinged stones in my collection than I can count, and all because along the way they were dropped, or fell off a table (or my cat decided they were balls and batted them around the room before I could rescue them). The lesson here is to protect your crystals and stones by handling them carefully if you want a long and happy relationship with them! And if they break, don't panic. Your crystal will still have its innate qualities. The biggest problem is that now they will have that jagged edge, and sometimes they can

be sharp—cutting sharp. My friends and I keep bowls in our homes that house our broken crystals and stones. This way we can still benefit from their energy within the room they are kept. Another good idea is to place them in your potted plants or your garden to the benefit of your flora. They won't mind the sharp edges.

Some people believe that if your stone breaks it's because it had an overload of negative energy, and it's best to simply bury it or throw it away, especially with hematite. And I guess that's possible. I'm more inclined to believe it was from my own clumsiness, or my cat attacks! So, another thing I do is stick some of the broken pieces in a muslin bag and toss them in my bath. I believe the energy of the crystals infuses the water while I soak, and I find crystal baths relaxing and refreshing.

HEALING TECHNIQUES

There are many ways to utilize stones and crystals for healing. Basically, you need to keep your crystal near to you or the chakra center you are working through. It starts with cleansing and dedicating your crystal for its purpose. This is the part where you take a few moments, at the least, to hold your stone after it's been cleared, and focus your intent upon it, stating clearly in your mind or vocally what you expect from the stone. Then simply wear it every day, preferably near the area that needs attention. If it is for a head, neck, or upper-body problem, then a pendant would be the easy choice for

keeping your crystal close. Use a long cord or chain if your problem is heart related or has to do with issues such as grief or depression. In these cases, you want the stone to be nearer the heart center of your body. When you are working on disorders dealing with the bottom half of your body, then carrying it in your pocket is another easy solution. Bracelets made from the stone of your choice are good for ailments such as arthritis, carpel tunnel syndrome, and the like. Some people use surgical tape and will tape a flat stone to specific areas of their bodies in an effort to seek relief.

Another effective way, and one that I personally use, is to sleep with the crystals. Placing them under your pillow or behind your back, or simply holding one in your hand as you drift off, can offer amazing support to the physical body. The best thing to do is what is practical for you, because if it isn't practical, then you probably won't keep it near you long enough to help. The stones and crystals aren't instant miracle workers; their energy takes time to sync with yours. To do this, they need to be close to your physical body, and they should be worn or carried on a regular basis.

An alternative method for using your crystals is by lying inside a crystal grid for a period of time. A half hour or so is adequate for this type of healing. To begin, you need to set out several crystals in an elongated pattern around the area you will be lying within. Some people prefer to align their crystals on their beds for more comfort, while others prefer a simple mat on the floor. This choice is nothing more than what makes you feel the most comfortable. If you wish to remain seated for this healing period, then place your stones in a circular pattern around the area where you will be seated, whether on the floor or in a chair. You may wish to play a CD of soft, natural sounds or soothing New Age music to help you relax your spirit during this ritual.

Now, to set up your grid you need to use at least four stones, one for each of the directions – north, south, east, and west, or as I prefer, eight. Then you can place an extra crystal in between the four cardinal points to form a more complete energy circuit. Clear quartz crystals or striated selenite wands are good choices for general healing purposes. You could also choose several stones

that are associated with the area of your body that needs work; for instance, rose quartz or green aventurine if you are looking to heal a heart chakra problem. You might choose to surround yourself with purple amethyst points if you are looking to reduce headaches or even enhance your own inner psychic awareness. The choice of stones is up to you and should either be clear or white for general healing or stress-reducing purposes, or crystals of color that associate with the chakra you are aiming your healing toward.

After placing your stones in a surrounding pattern, simply step inside and be seated, or lie down in the center of your ring of stones. If you have previous experience with yoga or any form of meditation, then go with what you know. If you have no experience, then you can simply start by relaxing and taking a few deep breaths, breathing in through the nostrils, and releasing slowly through your mouth. On your intake breath, imagine that you are bringing into your body clean, fresh air that will revitalize and strengthen your spirit. As you exhale, think about letting go of any tension or stress you may be holding on to. Do this several times until you feel relaxed. You can breathe normally at this point; just try to keep your breathing slow and steady. Next, I suggest turning your attention to the reason you are performing this exercise. If it is to reduce stress and tension in your life, then feel the energy of the stones entering your body with each slow, steady breath you take. Inhale this energy, taking it deep into your lungs, holding it for a few seconds, and releasing all the spent emotions that no longer serve you. Take your time and focus on breathing in the positive energy surrounding you and letting go of all the negative energy that was held inside. Find yourself growing more at ease and peaceful as you continue this process. Relax and let that smile cross your face as you begin to feel the uplifting serenity that is growing inside you. Close your eyes and open yourself to the rhythm of the crystal's vibrations as they penetrate your physical body. You can also mentally envision them as pulsing with celestial energy gently washing over your spirit, like soft ocean waves on a white sandy shore. The trick is to simply be in the moment and feel the natural energy in which you are immersed. Allow it to strengthen your spirit, clear your auric field, and open your chakras, restoring them to a balanced state.

You can specifically work on each individual chakra center if you wish. Some people like doing a chakra cleansing and alignment on a periodic basis to help them feel their best. For this you place the appropriate stone over each of the chakras and focus on clearing and strengthening each energy center in turn. Start by gathering the stones you are going to work with, one for each chakra center, and hold them in your hands. You could place the crystals for the three lower chakras in your left hand and hold the other four stones in your right hand.

Next, lie down and get comfortable. Start focusing your attention on your breathing. When doing this exercise, you are physically regulating your breath and slowing your pulse rate. As above, start by breathing slowly and deeply, inhaling the pure, clean air, holding it a few seconds, and then exhaling the spent, negative, energy with each exhale. This will allow you to reach a deeper-focused state of mind, one that will lead you in attuning with your crystal. When you are feeling as though you are ready, take the appropriate crystals and lay them atop the lower chakra centers. You could use a black or red stone to lay upon your lower pelvic region, then an orange one over your lower naval, and yellow over the mid-stomach area. Then place a green or pink stone over your heart. Now, place a blue stone over your throat, purple over the third eye, and clear or white stone on the floor or bed at the top of your head. Once you have the corresponding crystals on the chakra centers of your body, you are set to relax more deeply.

I prefer to begin at the top and work my way down, believing that the universal energy flows into my spirit body from the crown chakra center. Many prefer to start at the first, root chakra and work their way up to the crown. Choose whichever method feels right to you. Simply reverse the following process when performing this ritual.

Starting with the crown or head chakra, imagine a brilliant white light coming from out of nowhere and streaming in through your head. Imagine it clearing away any dark spots or attachments that may be hovering over your head. See the chakra as whirling free and clear, spinning its energy to a rhythmic motion, and begin to simply know that it is functioning properly. You can envision a large, brilliant diamond bursting with a spiritual white light, shining out and surrounding you in its glow. Cleansing in the crown chakra can help relieve headaches and upper-brain and memory issues. Think of this and take a deep breath, inhaling the light energy.

Next, move on to the third-eye chakra and envision this brilliant white light streaming down into the purple-colored vortex located between your eyes. Envision it bringing light into the darkness, clearing out any debris or negative attachments that are found clogging up the natural spinning rhythm of this energy center. As your third-eye center is clearing, imagine your vision opening to the inner realms of your mind, awakening your intuitive sense. See the purple color, pure and clear, like a quality amethyst. Your goal is to clarify this purple energy. Allow the light energy to swirl around this chakra, energizing it. When you feel this is done, take a deep breath, enjoy this cleanse, and prepare to move on.

Focus your attention on the next chakra down. Now the white light is coming down through your head, passing through your brain and third-eye chakra center and heading toward your throat. The color here is deep blue and the light is flooding your throat, picking out any dark matter or blockages that may have been causing problems. As the light filters and cleanses this energy center, see the beauty of cobalt-blue glass filtering the light. Know that you can now speak your own truth, allowing yourself freedom of expression. Clearing this center can also help increase your creativity. Feel the crystal-clear beauty of the blue in your mind and, breathing deeply, enjoy this thought for a moment before moving on to your next chakra.

Continue seeing the light moving in through the heart chakra. The light filters through any murky discolorations and clears this chakra. Envision the purity of the finest emerald, the size of your fist. See an interior light come to life inside your chest and glow, spreading a feeling of love and peace. Let this serenity enter your spirit, filling your soul and healing your body. With a cleansing here,

you are able to reduce emotional and physical pain, release regrets, and open your heart to love in all its forms. Once again, take a moment to experience this emotional release. Taking a deep breath, clear your mind and prepare to move on.

As the light moves into the yellow solar plexus area, follow its path. As it enters the stomach region of your body, imagine any muddiness that exists to disperse. The light is breaking down all sluggish detritus that has accumulated, dispersing it into the nether regions of space and time. As this happens, the yellow color takes on a bright glow, like the sun. Feel its warmth radiating throughout your body. Know that any stomach issues or sadness that once held sway is now clearing out, falling away from your spirit. Breathe deeply and relax in the joy and happiness from this bright-yellow glow that now emanates from this region of your body.

Moving on to the sacral chakra, allow the energetic white light to wash over and through the orange color you envision covering your navel. Picture the muddiness and any darkness pooling together and being wiped out by this light. As it erases any negativity swimming around, you can envision this chakra center beginning to glow brightly, a beautifully lit, amber-colored orange. With its clearing you begin to feel stronger, more vital and able to take on the world. Breathe in this newfound inner strength that has been made available to you. Relish the return of this energy and zest for life and know that problems with your organs of elimination are fading away, as well as backaches and pains. Then relax and take a deep breath before moving your focus to the first chakra center.

As you visualize your root chakra, see the color red. This is your foundation in life, the solid base you stand upon. Here you are rooted to the Earth from which you came. With eyes closed, see the light of the universe as it enters this center located in your pelvic region. Let it stir up any debris that has fallen here, and send it out and away from your body. Watch as this great light clears away the shadows and negative energies that were slowing down the natural swirling rhythm of this chakra. The red light begins to glow like a crystal-clear ruby, lit from within by a miniature sun. As this chakra is cleansed you will feel stabilized in your life, no longer at the mercy of fate. Feel your inner power return and grow, protecting you from the slings and arrows of life events. Problems that you may have had in the lower part of your body can now begin to heal as you allow the energy of the Divine to reach into your core being and spread throughout your body. Breathe deeply and calmly, and relax. Take a moment and feel the elevation of your spirit as your chakras have been cleansed. When you are finished, take the stones from their positions on your body, place them aside, and sit up. Show gratitude and thank God, or whatever divinity you believe in, for his/her assistance in this process. At this point you should be feeling better, clearer, happier, and hopefully, in less pain. When you are finished, it's a good idea to cleanse your stones and put them away for the next time you want to perform this exercise.

INTRODUCING THE HEALING CRYSTALS AND STONES

Before we start the alphabetical listing and description of each crystal or stone and their metaphysical qualities, I would like to begin with some general associations between the stones, according to their color. Most often it's their natural pigment that often links them with the various chakra points. You will find that crystals in these color groupings will tend to have very similar traits. When you understand the similarities within a color grouping, it then follows that you will find it easier to substitute one stone for another. This is important because you will not always be able to find a particular stone. You need to realize that most of the crystals and stones sold in shops today, or even online, are coming from different countries and, of course, different mines. There are many factors that contribute to their local availability at any one time. Therefore, you may not be able to find that certain stone you wanted, but by knowing its base characteristics, you can easily find another stone that will work on the same problem. Of course, each individual stone will naturally have its own specific attributes, and you will still need to intuit which one harmonizes with your own personal rhythm.

Please, do not feel guilty about replacing one stone or crystal for another. It's simply a matter of the crystal's frequency that makes it work. For instance, I've had people come in looking for moldavite. Sometimes it will be out of stock. This crystal, coming from Moldavia, is rare and in limited quantity, making the pricing higher than most other stones its size. Whenever we are out of stock, or a customer balks at the cost, I always suggest tektite as a substitute because it too is formed from meteor crashes and has very similar traits to the moldavite. It's priced a lot less because it is found in various places around the globe and isn't as rare. The primary difference between the two stones is that moldavite is bottle green in color, and the tektite is generally black; however, they both work on all the chakras due to their higher level of frequency, and both were formed from meteoric impact.

Another time I had someone come into the shop looking for green fuchsite. Unfortunately, it was on back order at the time, so I asked the lady what she wanted it for. After a moment's hesitation, she admitted to hearing it could help contact the devic realms. She was working in a corner of her yard and was fashioning it into a fairy garden and hoped that by placing a few of those stones around, it might help attract fairies, in spirit if not in reality. This customer felt it was something she needed to do. I suggested trying tree agate and aventurine, since they also can help connect with the nature realms, as well as basic quartz crystal, mostly because it can sparkle, and fairies are supposed to like that! I proposed the quartz because she could program her desire for wishing or welcoming fairies into her garden. She left the shop with a quartz and some tree agate, though I felt she was not convinced. A few weeks later she came in again and, upon seeing me, broke into a smile. I asked her how she was. She related that after placing the stones in her garden, her plants seemed to be coming up better than she had expected. The fairies had yet to show themselves, but when working in her garden she felt as though they might just be watching! Then, giving me a sly look and a wink, she walked away. I can't say she factually attracted the fairies, but the stones she used obviously made her plants happy.

The point is that for whatever reason, it is always okay to find a substitute if the specific crystal you are seeking is unattainable. Let your intuition lead the way and simply search for stones with similar properties. The next few pages will show you the traits held by the various color groupings.

CRYSTALS BY COLOR

Clear and White Stones

These are the stones that associate with the crown chakra located at the top of the head. Their energy works through this seventh chakra point, illuminating and lifting the spirit within. In healing, these stones are used for ailments or diseases located in the head, including mental as well as physical illnesses.

Most of the white or clear crystals are especially good for attuning yourself to the higher realms in meditation. They help you align with the universal creative forces, spirit guardians, angels, and even those of the nature spirit and fairy realms. When kept under your pillow or held in your hand, these stones allow you to drift off and fall asleep in a peaceful state of mind. They enhance your rest and can bring clarity to your dreams. The clear and white crystals are also great for meditation, as they help open you to the possibilities this energy carries. These are great stones to use when connecting to the creative and healing powers in the universe. They assist in drawing these forces into your soul and allowing them to enlighten any darkness that lurks in the shadows. Remember, as each of us possesses our own unique rhythm, so do the crystals. That is why certain stones may work better for one person than another. It's always best to go to the stone that draws your attention. Trust your instincts when choosing a crystal for healing. The spirit usually knows what the brain has yet to learn!

Yellow and Orange Stones

The vibrational rhythm of stones in the yellow to orange family of colors resonates with the second and third chakras, which energize the solar plexus and stomach area of the body. In general, they work on helping align these energy centers, alleviating problems within the physical body that are connected to the overall digestive tract, the sexual or reproductive organs, and those of detoxification and elimination. Working with these crystals allows you to help the body heal itself by clearing the blockages that inhibit or retard the proper digestion of food, the source of fuel for the body.

These crystals are also useful when attempting to lift depression and gloomy moods. They are great for bringing self-confidence back into the spirit, energizing that inner core of being that helps you realize that you do have what it takes! When clearing or cleansing the lower chakras, you can rid yourself of self-doubt and insecurities. Blockages and sluggish pathways in this area of the body tend to keep a person feeling drained—unable to fight for their rights, or stand tall and be motivated. Meditating with, and wearing, the yellow and orange stones will give that little extra lift needed to propel you into the world, putting that little bounce back into your step as you walk through the day with more confidence. Naturally, each stone has its own special affinity for different problems; the key is to find the stone that attunes to your spirit.

Pink Stones

The pink crystals vibrate to the rhythm of love and peace and are naturally attuned to the heart chakra when used in healing meditations or rituals. Even though the heart chakra is thought to vibrate to the frequency of the color green, most of the pink-colored stones are also associated with this fourth chakra energy center. It is through here that the loving force permeates the auric field, allowing for a calming and tranquil feeling to flow throughout the body. That is one of the reasons rose quartz has been so often recommended for use with children. It exerts such a palliative and peaceful energy on the spirit of the children that it helps them in times of stress and frustration.

Another aspect of pink stones is their association with universal love and compassion for others. These are both qualities that children need to learn and incorporate into their nature as they grow into adulthood, if we want them to become higher-minded beings when they reach maturity.

When used in healing sessions, rituals, or meditations, pink stones help with all heart-related issues, from repairing tissue and aiding the circulatory system to helping detoxify some major organs. Pink stones are also excellent at mitigating anxiety- and stress-related issues by offering an energetic healing of the auric field surrounding the body. Naturally, each type of stone has its own vibratory pattern that will associate with different parts of the body.

Red Stones

The red crystals rhythmically vibrate to the root and sacral chakras. Their natural quality is generally considered invigorating and fortifying. They can awaken the base energy located at the bottom of the spine and allow you to grow both physically and spiritually. These stones are great at revitalizing a sluggish system, adding that little bit of fire energy to the auric field. They help increase passion and vigor for everyday pursuits by providing the driving factor needed to get things accomplished.

Working through the root chakra, they also help stabilize a flighty personality by helping to keep your feet rooted to the Earth. That is why they work so well as a grounding stone, anchoring you to the here and now, focusing on the actuality of a given situation. Red stones also have a warming effect on the body and are generally considered stimulating to the circulatory system, sexual prowess, and the reproductive organs. The motivating energy of these stones makes them useful in manifesting your desires in life, whether working on a project or accomplishing a goal. Wearing this color of crystal will help you achieve your objective by aiding you with stamina and endurance. Since red is also associated with the blood, these stones are good for working on blood-related illnesses. However, you should be careful as their stimulating effect could work against some things, such as hypertension. Best to use black or dark crystals when your system is already overstimulated.

Blue Stones

Crystals and stones with blue hues flow gently with the rhythm of the throat or fifth chakra. Their general characteristics are calming and cooling, while enhancing self-expression and creativity. The blue stones work well in cooling down overly energetic people and those who can't seem to stay focused. They are believed to enhance creativity and artistic thoughts and are frequently suggested for any type of artist. They are especially helpful when writing, creatively or for a class paper. They are useful for those who make speeches, or salesmen giving a "pitch," as they work through the throat chakra, enhancing your ability to speak clearly and make yourself understood. When seeking clarification or inner knowledge of a situation, blue crystals will help open our inner psyche to the stored knowledge hidden in our subconscious. The paler-colored blue stones, such as celestite and blue lace agate, are considered excellent stones for stress release. They send calming vibrations throughout the auric field, moderating the tension that keeps us agitated or on edge.

Physically, blue stones are helpful with throat-related injuries, blockages, and illnesses. Worn frequently, they can assist the body with stuttering and other speech impediments. A blue crystal is a good choice to hold when meditating on communications with other realms or trying to increase spiritual connections. Of course, each blue stone carries its own specific rhythm, and you simply need to find the right stone that works for you.

Aqua and Turquoise Stones

The crystals in this group typically relate to the throat and heart chakras and sing to the emotional nature of our auric fields. These stones are sometimes combinations of two varieties that grow well together in their crystalline natures, harmonically blending into their own unique natural wonder. There are exceptions to this, such as turquoise, some aquamarines, and other stones whose color simply is a merging of the colors blue and green.

Most of these stones work to harmonize the auric field, allowing for the free flow of energy from the heart to the throat and upper chakras. Their blended influence is generally helpful for the lungs and chest area of the body. They are used in meditations to help attune to the emotional nature, clearing out the blockages that divide us and opening the heart to give and receive love in all its forms. They have a calming effect on the spirit, bringing a feeling of benevolence to the wearer. They can also inspire creativity in the artist, encouraging and enabling him or her to give to the world their own sense of truth and beauty. Physically, they cover a range of healing attributes from the throat and neck to the heart and upper digestive tract, depending on the dominance of which color, the blue or green, is more prominent. The blue stones will work more effectively with throat and speech issues, while the green crystals would be more beneficial for the heart and lungs.

Green Stones

Green crystals and stones are linked to the heart chakra and the melody of universal love. Their special qualities work to open the spirit to accept the divine force of love that surrounds all of creation. They teach our spirit to grow and help us reach toward the higher realms where divinity resides. They also allow us to empathize with each other so that we may attain that elusive feeling of unity with our fellow man. The green crystals are excellent at showing our spirits that love is the best solution to any problem we think we have. Through this loving emotion, many will find solace after long periods of grief, learning that the loss of a loved one, whether from a separation of ways or a death, isn't the end. We learn to move on yet still carry that feeling of love, knowing the emotion was, and is, a reality unto itself and will always exist. Green crystals and stones can clear blockages in the heart chakra so this energy can flow up and down the meridian lines, bringing a sense of peace and joy to the spirit within.

Physically the green crystals work on the circulatory system, strengthening the heart, lungs, liver, and kidneys, helping to detoxify these organs. An added benefit of green stones is that some of them are often considered inherently lucky. It's believed that when they are carried about, they attract abundance and prosperity into your life.

Purple and Violet Stones

The natural rhythm of the purple and violet stones is generally tuned to the higher vibratory patterns of the universe, similar to the white and clear crystals. These stones are sympathetically linked with the third-eye and crown chakras, working to expand the mind, opening it to new ideas and realizations. They help you achieve deeper states of meditation, aiding healing on a mental level. They can elevate the psyche to expand and grow, aligning itself with the universal consciousness. The purple and violet crystals can offer protection from negative attachments and spirits. They help ward off many evils sent your way, especially the harmful mental outburst of others who are angry. The abusive or pessimistic outburst of other people can affect your auric field. It's as if they are throwing darts of destruction into your energetic sphere, causing blockages or tears. Sometimes it can feel like their actions and words are hitting and hurting your spirit, like rocks being thrown at your soul. Purple crystals have the ability to deflect this negativity, blocking it from entering your personal space. This is how they act as stones of protection.

Physically, most of the crystals of the purple ray are used in healings that deal with the general area of the head, such as migraines, concussions, and mental disorders, as well as issues related to sight and hearing. Some of the stones, such as amethyst, are believed to help you fight off addictions, particularly alcohol.

Gold and Brown Stones

The colors of these crystals align them with the sacral and solar plexus chakras in healings, though some will work also on the root chakra. These are the energy centers that help us define who we are and what we stand for. This is where we learn self-confidence and find our own personal courage to face what life throws our way. Gold and brown stones are also centering stones that help us find balance in our lives and emotions. They have a stabilizing effect on the spirit. Whereas the black and red stones are for grounding, the brown stones give us the strength to stand that ground, maintaining the stamina needed to see us through. In general, the brown crystals help us face reality by focusing our attention in the present. They help us see things as they are, not as we want them to be, and offer a sense of security and steadfastness in the wake of emotional storms that may come our way as we travel through life.

Since these colors are just deeper, darker shades of the yellow and orange spectrum, they tend to carry similar vibrations, though perhaps of a more somber nature. They help clear blockages and imperfections in the auric field in the lower chakra spectrum—the first, second, and third—that in turn can aid most issues that affect this area, such as the gonads, ovaries, stomach, colon, and lower back, and they assist in general pain relief.

Black Stones

The deep vibrational levels of the black crystals are tuned into the energies of the Earth and are protective and grounding. Their relationship is with the root chakra, and they harmonize well with red crystals and stones. Most black crystals have the innate ability to clear and deflect harmful and damaging energy from entering your auric field or attaching itself to you. Many people find that merely holding on to a black stone will calm their fears when facing the unknown, and they are a favorite of ghost hunters when seeking to communicate with spirits on the other side of life. This is because of the belief that the black stones can deflect the harmful energy that may emanate from departed spirits who are lost in a mist of their own negativity, as well as defend them from any evil lurking in the shadows. Be mindful though that some, such as obsidian, when polished in the form of a flat disc or ball, are used in scrying (peering into an object for the purpose of seeing into the future). Black obsidian can also be used to communicate with the dead, so if you are a sensitive person looking for protection, black tourmaline or onyx may be a better choice for you. As with all crystals, you must choose the black stone that vibrates in frequency with your own natural energy. In general, I feel that the black stones tend to work more on an etheric level than a physical one in healing.

The similarity of traits with crystals in the same color families is a helpful guide when seeking to make substitutions. As stated previously, you won't always find the crystal or stone you think you must have for any specific problem. By using this information, you will more easily find a substitute crystal or stone that will work for you. Open your mind and prepare to learn the qualities of what I believe to be the more fundamental and popular crystals and stones. They have been arranged in alphabetical order for ease of use.

CRYSTAL LISTINGS

BLUE LACE AGATE

This heavenly blue crystal is associated with the **THROAT CHAKRA** and is useful in clearing blockages in that area of the body.

The tranquility of this agate is easy to feel. Its calming influence gives you the clarity of thought needed to realize that whatever is bothering you will pass in time. It helps you look at situations with more composure. If part of the problem is feeling stifled or not heard, it helps you express yourself in a true and concise manner. Blue lace agate is a stone of communication that aids your spirit in articulating your core beliefs. By improving your fluency in speech, you find that others are more willing to listen to what you have to say. The serenity offered by this stone also helps you unburden yourself from many of the little upsets encountered in daily life. When used in meditations, it can open the aura to higher spiritual influences. Attuning yourself to these levels can help in many ways, from creatively exploring your own beliefs to sharing them for the benefit of others. Though not normally used to combat depression, it helps you face hard facts with a graceful understanding. This, in turn, can lift those dark feelings, allowing the light to reenter your life and to renew hope deep inside your soul.

Physically, this stone should be worn around the neck when used in healings for disorders such as laryngitis, speech impediments, sore throats, and thyroid problems. It's especially helpful for the tension that builds in the upper shoulders from time spent bending over a desk or computer. It can also work on the energetic meridians that affect the lymphatic and nervous system when used in healing meditations.

This agate is a banded form of chalcedony, a microcrystalline variety of quartz. Discovered in southwestern Africa, it is also found in the US and India.

MOSS AGATE

This multishaded variety of green
agate works primarily through the
HEART CHAKRA, bringing a harmony
or balance to the entire system.

I t has an affinity with Earth energy and the natural world, which includes plants and animals. It is one of the recommended stones to use in your garden, or even a potted plant, when you want to encourage growth and vitality. This crystal is also often suggested for veterinarians and those who work closely with animals, especially pet owners who wish to commune more closely with their companions. It's simply a good choice for anyone working with nature. This includes farmers as well as botanists, tree trimmers, or even park rangers. The natural earth essence of this crystal harmonizes well with any field that includes plants or animals.

Moss agate is a go-to crystal when dark moods become a problem, by adding an optimistic boost to the spirit, thereby helping to lift depressive thoughts. It's a cooling stone, often worn or carried for its anti-inflammatory action on the body, as well as helping to calm down those with hot tempers! For this reason, it can help with arthritis, rheumatism, and skin inflammations. Another trait attributed to this stone is its ability to relieve stress and tension held in the back.

Physically, moss agate works on regulating the circulation and the lymphatic glands, and helping the body eliminate harmful elements through detoxification. Essentially working through the heart chakra, it can aid those recovering from heart attacks as it encourages cell regeneration. Moss agate is also considered a lucky stone that can attract money and prosperity to the person who carries it. It's known as a stone of new beginnings and is good to have around when you are embarking on new ventures.

Moss agate is a silicon dioxide mineral that can be found in many places, including India, South America, and Canada.

TREE AGATE

Generally associated with the
HEART CHAKRA, tree agate
is another good choice for
gardeners, farmers, and those
who work in nature.

T he color of green, branch-like markings over white is what differentiates this stone from other dendritic agates. The patterns are reminiscent of trees or ferns; hence its name. It has a natural affinity for communing with tree spirits and plants for those who wish to meditate outdoors. Most agates work in slow and steady ways, vibrating to the deep rhythms of the Earth, and are, therefore, helpful in stabilizing the emotional nature. Many people find solace and serenity when holding their stone as they walk through a wooded area, letting the energy of the surrounding landscape envelope and cleanse their spirits of negativity. Crystals with more white on the surface are used in meditations or healings, working through the crown chakra. These agates help our minds expand and see the oneness of all life in the universe, the union of the realms—animal, mineral, and vegetable. When we learn to accept this notion, we grow a little closer to the universal truths, a little closer to our union with the divine.

Tree agate can help the body in self-healing with issues related to the heart, blood vessels, and capillaries. It helps balance the nervous system and can bring relief to tension- or stress-related backaches. It also helps a loving energy take root in our soul, opening our hearts to give and receive a universal kindness and empathy toward our fellow creatures, man and animal alike. In this way it balances our emotions and brings a sense of stability and confidence to our feelings, allowing us to socialize and connect with others more freely.

Tree agate is another silicon dioxide mineral with inclusions of iron or manganese that give it its distinctive markings. It normally comes from South America and India.

AMAZONITE

The restful color of this
crystal can be very quieting
to those under duress.

It works through both the heart and throat chakras. The blue-toned crystals align more to the throat area, while the ones with more of a green hue fall under the influence of the heart center. Amazonite soothes the emotional nature, healing old wounds and restoring a sense of peace and serenity. It can help one release fear and other negative emotions when it is worn or carried. Its cooling vibration can bring a balance to those with overheated natures, people with a tendency to anger quickly. It is also helpful when used to quell depressive thoughts and brooding tendencies. It is one of those stones you can meditate on when learning to speak your own truth or attempting to find your own path. It can be equally good to hold when doing positive affirmations as it helps the spirit manifest its desires into reality. This stone is one of the lucky crystals. It's believed to draw abundance and prosperity into your life when kept close. It's a good choice for those who like to commune with nature and seek to contact the devic or fairy realms.

Physically, amazonite can work well for the pains of arthritis and rheumatism, lessening them by dampening the inflammatory response of the body. It is also a good choice to wear for muscle spasms and strains. I personally wear an amazonite chip bracelet along with a magnetic copper band to quell wrist pain whenever I type. Made into an elixir and poured on a poultice, it has been used for treating rashes and blisters. It aids in cellular regeneration and can help stabilize metabolic disorders. It helps healing with issues related to the throat, thyroid, lungs, and heart.

Amazonite is a potassium silicate mineral with copper and can be found in South America, North America, India, and Russia.

AMBER

Amber has a sunny
energy that acts like a
tonic for the auric field.

I t lightens the entire meridian system, bringing with it a natural feeling of joy and happiness. It can work on all the chakra centers when used in a healing ritual by clearing away harmful energies and attachments to the spirit body and energy centers. This allows the body to regulate itself and restore balance to its physical systems. Due to its coloring, amber is considered a potent cleanser of the solar plexus, aiding with digestion and balancing the metabolism. In ancient times it was used to help clear infections and wounds. It is a good choice for clearing the lymphatic system and has also been used as a remedy for teething and toothaches, but one must be careful not to let babies chew on the pieces as they are more liable to swallow or choke on them.

Though technically not a crystal, this resin is listed along with the crystals because it has traditionally been used for its healing benefits as much as its use in jewelry. The largest deposit of amber was originally found in the Baltic region (Baltic amber) and is thought to be approximately forty million years or older. This is considered the best grade of amber, and the pricing reflects that. True ancient amber was also discovered in the Dominican Republic and is currently being mined at that location. However, much of what is on the market today can be copal, which, though also a resin, is much younger in age and ranges from about 250,000 to 100,000 years or older. Unfortunately, that isn't enough time for the chemical reactions to take place within the resin to chemically distinguish it as amber. I believe that copal has similar healing properties to amber, only to a slightly lesser extent or strength.

AMETHYST

This purple gem is considered a highly protective and purifying stone.

Generally associated with the third-eye and crown chakras, it's great at blocking harmful energies from attaching themselves and disrupting your entire auric field. It can also be used to protect you from thieves and liars, deflecting these negative energies. In focused introspection, it helps open the third eye and awaken your psychic senses and increase your natural intuition when it is worn daily. A very spiritual crystal, amethyst is a great choice when used to commune with your spirit guides. Certain Buddhist monks use amethyst prayer malas for the ability to enter a deeper state of meditation. Amethyst encourages a calming peace that can assist you in clearing oppressive thoughts from your mind and bringing about a better understanding of situations that are bothering you. It is the choice crystal for many people when fighting addictive behaviors, especially alcoholism.

Physically, this stone is often used to treat headaches and migraines. When lying down, place a crystal on either side of your temples to bring relief. It supports the pituitary gland and hormone balance. Additionally, it is used in healings for nerve disorders, tinnitus, and some brain imbalances. It's a great crystal to use for restful sleep as it helps dispel nightmares. It's the stone my sister places under her pillow whenever she experiences a restless night. She swears it allows her to fall gently off and sleep till morning. It's also a good idea to keep amethyst in a sick room near an ill person as it helps clear the air of negativity while sending out soothing vibes that aid rest and recuperation.

A silicon dioxide mineral, a variety of quartz, amethyst gets its color from the combination of the iron and aluminum trace minerals within. It is found in many places, including North and South America, Africa, Europe, and Russia.

ANGELITE

The melody that angelite sings
is one of peaceful awareness,
benevolence, and communion.

I ts calming and enlightening influence works through the top three chakras from the throat to the crown. This crystal is often used in prayerful meditations when one is trying to contact guardian spirits or others in the angelic realms. Soothing to the soul, this crystal increases awareness of the higher realms while improving receptivity to telepathic and empathetic communications, both from those on Earth and those who have ascended to higher planes of existence. It stimulates your own rhythmic frequency to help your energetic essence tune into those higher realms. It can awaken the inner awareness that lets you see the subliminal patterns in your life. Angelite is also good for encouraging lucid dreaming when placed under your pillow at night. While emanating a blissful, calming serenity, angelite cleanses your soul of negative energies while filling it with celestial light. It aids the equilibrium of the auric field when used in rituals to clear and balance the chakra centers. It works well when used in meditations to open the third-eye or the crown chakra, allowing the celestial or Universal Light to stream through and spread all over the meridian system, clearing away debris and negativity.

This stone is often used in healings that deal with any throat-related disorders, including the thyroid gland, and is also credited with aiding kidney functions and fluid imbalances in the body. Because of its calcium content it's believed to help increase bone density and assist with the healing of broken bones. Some find it useful in dealing with the pain of arthritis and other inflammatory conditions due to the cooling effect it has on the body.

Angelite is a calcium sulfate mineral most commonly found in Peru, but in other places as well, such as Mexico, portions of North Africa, and parts of Europe.

APATITE

Apatite helps you with spiritual growth,
especially when used in meditations
that seek union with the divine source.

L ike Joseph's coat of many colors, apatite can also be found in a variety of colors, from white to brown; however, we will be describing the blue and turquoise variation of this crystal. It works well on the throat and third-eye chakras, stimulating your inner senses as it widens your perspectives in life. On a more conventional level, it helps you organize your thoughts and speak more clearly when trying to get your point across. Working through the throat chakra, it is a good stone for teachers, sales persons, and those in the acting profession to carry about, as it promotes clarity of thought and confidence in speaking. The stones that are more turquoise or tending toward green in color will work through the heart chakra, bringing out emotional depth and lending passion to your speech. Apatite is also good at helping you see things with a rational mindset, which can be very beneficial to those who tend to overanalyze and worry themselves over the little things in life. In this way it helps calm your mind and to relieve some of that self-induced stress, so you can breathe easier and accomplish more.

The calcium content in apatite makes it a good choice to work with in healings for broken bones and strengthening the teeth. It's also a good stone to wear for arthritis and rheumatism as its cooling influence will help calm these inflammatory conditions while it supports the cartilage. I recommend wearing it in bracelet form or carrying a stone in your pocket if these conditions affect your hips or lower back.

Apatite is a calcium phosphate mineral that can be found in North and South America as well as Europe, Russia, and South Africa.

AQUAMARINE

This crystal's connection to the
water element gently washes over
your emotions in a soothing wave.

W orking through the throat and heart chakra, aquamarine aids those who are speaking, teaching, or lecturing for a living. It helps you find and form the right words to say in most situations. It's a cooling stone that comforts the spirit and balances the emotions when carried or worn. It's a good choice for those whose tempers tend to flare too quickly, because it cools down a fiery nature. Focusing on this crystal will help you modulate your voice and tone down angry thoughts. A good meditation or prayer stone, it helps with concentration on a higher level, finding the serenity needed to achieve that inner connection with your spirit guides. Aquamarine can also help increase your inner vision and expand your psychic awareness.

When worn as a necklace or pendant, it helps those with allergies, sore throats, laryngitis, or swollen glands. A few years ago, one of our customers bought an aquamarine chip necklace and wore it throughout the allergy season. She told us it had helped her tremendously. It didn't eradicate her allergies totally, but she said they were much easier to control with simple over-the-counter remedies. In the past, my own allergic response has been mild compared to many of my friends, but now I too wear an aquamarine necklace in the spring and fall and rarely experience any symptoms! Aquamarine is also beneficial for the thyroid gland and can be useful in relieving coughing and throat spasms.

An aluminum beryllium silicate, aquamarine is one of the varieties of beryl that gets its color from trace minerals – from light-blue to greenish-blue shades. It can be found around the world, in North America and South America, Africa, Europe, and the Ural Mountains of Russia.

BLUE ARAGONITE

Mainly working through the **THROAT CHAKRA** on the physical level, this heavenly blue crystal also influences the **THIRD-EYE CHAKRA** by opening the psyche to inner visions.

I t is a great tool to use in meditations increasing psychic perceptions and abilities and the depth of happier emotional states. The secret is to truly feel the connection, or harmony, between this crystal and you. And that's an easy thing to do since it gives off a comforting and welcoming vibration to most people. Working with blue aragonite helps tune you into your emotional health, while helping to clear out harmful blockages in your auric field. It's also considered a particularly good stone to work with in Reiki healings or touch therapies. Blue aragonite is useful for whole-body healing layouts as it strengthens the emotional body to deal with the problems at hand. It can help release the inner fears that hold you back from expressing yourself or that have held you captive to habits and situations no longer working for you. It assists you in moving forward in your life, and once again looking to the future with a renewed sense of hope.

It can be of assistance when the intent is to commune with angelic beings or guardian spirits. Its calming influence helps when trying to obtain a sense of oneness with the universe.

Physically, aragonite works well for throat-related ailments, speech impediments, and respiratory and lung issues. It helps cool the inflammation of sore throats, easing the pain. It's a great stone to use for relief from worry and stress, dissipating the tension held in your muscles, allowing you to relax. It's useful in meditations focused on breathing or breath work.

A calcium carbonate mineral, aragonite is found in various colors and is mined around the world, including the US, China, Spain, and Sicily.

BROWN ARAGONITE

Normally sold as small *star* clusters,
these are higher-vibrational crystals
that help stabilize the auric field as they
infuse it with healing vibrations.

I t might not magically win the lottery for you, but its energetic crystalline composition, when properly tuned into your own, can help find that extra cash when needed. It is also recommended for those in business to attract more customers. Aventurine can also be a good choice for gardeners as it has a special relationship with the devic (fairy and nature spirits) realms and is believed to attract them into your yard. Even if you don't believe in the fairy realms, it is a good idea to place some around your garden as the stone's Earth energy can encourage healthy growth in the plants living there. Due to its green color, aventurine is associated with the heart chakra. Working through this center, it can lift your spirit, instilling you with a sense of happiness and inner freedom as well as aiding self-confidence.

Physically, aventurine can strengthen the vitality, renewing a sense of vigor when you are feeling worn out and old. It's also considered a general healing crystal because it can clear the auric field of negative emotions that dampen your health. It's a good choice for healings that deal with the heart, lungs, and liver, and inflammations that can erupt on the skin, such as rashes, ulcers, and the like. Its energetic influence assists in stabilizing the circulation and the metabolism, allowing for the free flow of energy as the body works to heal itself.

This variety of silicon dioxide mineral can contain trace inclusions of fuchsite, iron, or mica, which give some stones their fascinating sparkle. Aventurine can also be found in natural colors of red or blue. These stones will have properties associated with the throat and root chakra according to their color. It can be found in Brazil, Russia, and India.

AZURITE

The deep cobalt-blue color of
azurite is a striking contrast to most
other naturally blue-toned stones.

T hough linked to the throat chakra, it is a great stone to clear and open the third eye, allowing for the growth of psychic abilities and intuition. A strong healing stone, its frequency can clear the auric field around all the upper chakras. This can bring about a keener inner vision and understanding of circumstances, as well as the emotional effects they place upon you when you are feeling ill or out of sorts. It can help calm those inner voices that repeat self-defeating thoughts that tend to hold you back from expanding your reach into the world. Using this stone in meditations can open new pathways for a more enlightened state of being, enlarging your horizons and assisting you in learning to release your inner spirit. It's a good choice when attempting to journey through the astral realms to further educate your soul. It is also used when trying to communicate with those beings in the higher realms, opening a link to your spirit guides. Azurite is also believed to help heal holes or tears in the auric field, strengthening it, and so it can be worn for protection against psychic attacks or spirit attachments.

Physically resonating with all three upper chakras enables this crystal to help with such disorders as tinnitus, headaches, memory, and other neural- or brain-related problems. Working through the throat chakra, it helps with the larynx and speech impediments. Azurite's cooling influence is also helpful for sore throats and inflammations. For some people it has been found useful in treating arthritis and angina.

This copper carbonate mineral can be found in various deposits around the world, including France, the US, Mexico, Russia, and Brazil. It is often found in mining deposits mixed with crystal malachite.

AZURITE-MALACHITE

This alluring combination of two copper carbonate crystals works primarily through the **HEART, THROAT, AND THIRD-EYE CHAKRAS**.

Y ou will find it great for use in meditations when you wish to open and develop your third eye. The deep cobalt blue of the azurite increases your inner awareness and helps activate natural psychic abilities. And the comingling of azurite and malachite helps open your consciousness to the bigger picture. While the deep-green malachite harmonizes with your emotional heart, the lovely blue azurite works on your logical mind, allowing you to view situations from a higher and wiser perspective.

This blend of stones is great for cleansing the meridians and clearing obstructions that can hold you back in life. Azurite-malachite assists in finding your own truth and gives you the courage to speak it clearly. In cleansing the chakras, it dissolves those attachments and blockages that can cause disease and illness, allowing the physical body to begin work on healing itself. The natural blending of these crystals makes them a good choice for any ailment related to the heart, lungs, and throat area. Together they are also supportive of the gall bladder, kidneys, spleen, and liver. Their copper content works well for the body that is afflicted by arthritis and rheumatism. This combination stone has many benefits that derive from its natural pairing, and it is also used for problems with the bones, teeth, headaches, and tinnitus. This is not a good stone to use in elixir form; simply keep it close or use it in healing meditations or rituals.

Azurite can also be found mixed with chryscolla, another member of the copper family. Preferable cleansing rituals for this crystal would be smudging, sun or moonlight, and lying near hematites to draw off any negativity. Essentially a variety of copper carbonate minerals, azurite-malachite is mined in many places, such as Africa, Russia, and Australia.

BLOODSTONE

Considered a great crystal for
purifying the body as well as the spirit,
bloodstone is a good general healing
crystal that has been used for centuries.

I t is normally associated with the heart and root chakra in healing layouts. Legend has it that the red inclusions (of hematite) were believed to have appeared at the Crucifixion, from the blood of Christ dripping onto the green jasper stones below. Historically, people would grind the stone, mix it with honey, and use the resulting paste to stanch the flow of blood. On the metaphysical level, bloodstones were used in times past to invoke the forces of nature in weather magic. They were also worn as amulets that could detect lies and untruths in the words of others.

Bloodstones have protective qualities that are useful in dispelling harmful obstructions in the auric field. By deflecting this negativity, they protect your aura and allow for the free flow of energy between the meridian points. This positive spiritual stream allows for self-healing to begin. When working through the root chakra, it makes for an excellent grounding stone, helping you focus on the realities of situations while giving you the strength you need to make hard decisions. It can help improve tendencies toward reactionary impulses, temper flare-ups, and the like, by grounding your emotional outbursts. Bloodstone can give you the ability to stop and think for a moment, counting to ten if need be, before your mood gets the better of you.

Working through the heart chakra, bloodstone energies are effective in purification and detoxification of the heart, liver, spleen, kidneys, and other organs of filtration. It helps fortify the immune system and is useful in any healing related to the blood stream and bone marrow.

Bloodstones are silicon dioxide minerals and a variety of chalcedony. They can be found in Brazil, India, North America, Australia, and China.

BORNITE
(Peacock Ore)

Often referred to as peacock ore,
bornite displays a metallic array
of colors that shimmer like the tail
feathers of the peacock.

This crystal carries an ethereal energy that allows it to work on all the chakra centers, a factor that makes it a good choice for meditations. Bornite is also considered a happy stone, one that will lift your spirits and knock away the doldrums when you keep it near. If you are looking for some joy in your life, carry it on a daily basis. Its effect is to bring a little light into the dark corners of the mind, releasing old fears and moodiness. It also clears out blockages and disharmonious energies in the auric field. The vibratory patterns of this stone can also be used to help cleanse a room of negative energies left by ill-tempered people. Leave it sitting out on top of your desk or a table in a room you share with others.

More of a mental or spiritual stone, bornite can still be used for healing the body. It can assist in regulating the electrolyte balances in the body as well as stabilizing the flow of adrenaline when used in Reiki or healing-grid layouts. It can be useful in regulating the metabolism when focused on in meditation. It's also believed to harmonize the cellular structure, which will aid in tissue regeneration and repair.

It is often confused with chalcopyrite, a chemically similar stone. Both are copper sulfide mineral ores that tarnish to displays of metallic color. The deeper blues, greens, and purples form naturally on bornite. Chalcopyrite tarnishes to more gold and yellow tones; however, when subjected to an acid wash, it will also produce the blues, greens, and purples of bornite. This stone is a copper iron sulfide mineral that can be found in many places, including the US and Central and South America.

CLEAR CALCITE

Shining like a melting icicle, clear
calcite is known for being a good
energy cleanser and amplifier and
is considered stimulating for the
entire auric field.

M ainly linked to the crown and third-eye chakras, it clears blockages and opens your psyche to the higher fields of spiritual energy available in the universe. This calcite helps drive you to reach the next level of your spiritual development. It can help you seek and find the root causes of your problems in life, bringing into the light that which we have hidden from ourselves out of fear or guilt. It is also used as a focusing tool to improve your natural psychic abilities. Calcite allows for spiritual and psychic growth through meditation. It helps remove the stagnant energy that can accumulate in the auric field when you pass this crystal over and around your body. Alternately, you can have someone else take this crystal and pass it around your physical form, focusing on clearing any blockages surrounding you.

Due to its calcium content, it is naturally used for skeletal and joint problems. It aids in the uptake of calcium into the bones as well, helping to dissolve calcifications. It equalizes the auric field, working from the crown chakra downward. Some people use it as an elixir, letting the crystal sit inside a glass of water overnight and then drinking the water the next day. Or you can wear it to help cleanse the organs of elimination, such as the bladder, kidneys, and intestines. It's useful in clearing up certain skin conditions when the calcite water is used in the form of a poultice placed over the skin irritation site.

Calcite is a calcium carbonate mineral that can be found in western Europe, France, Madagascar, Egypt, and the US. It comes in a variety of colors from clear to green, yellow, orange, brown, and blue.

BLUE CALCITE

With a translucent appearance, blue calcite is linked to the **THROAT AND THIRD-EYE CHAKRAS**.

L ike most blue stones, it has a calming effect and is a good choice to carry or wear when your nerves are frayed. It helps many with reducing the tension held in the neck and shoulders as it lessens these effects of stress. Blue calcite also helps calm hot tempers, tamping down on those feelings of anger or rage that flare when you're under duress. I normally recommend sleeping with one under your pillow as it helps calm the spirit through the night. It's also a good idea to carry one throughout the day to help keep yourself under control.

Working through the throat chakra, calcite can help you get your point across in well-spoken, thought-out exchanges of dialogue. It can help those who need to speak their own truth or feel they are often misunderstood. By opening and clearing disharmony in your upper chakras, it encourages rational thinking and speech. This, in turn, will help others to better understand your point of view. Students can benefit from blue calcite because it helps them not only focus on their studies but remember them as well.

Blue calcite is considered an energy amplifier, strengthening the aura while cleansing it.

Since calcium is the main component, this crystal works well with healing layouts for problems associated with the bones and joints, especially for the neck and the upper spine area. It is also used for most throat problems, such as laryngitis, sore throats, speech impediments, and the like. Blue calcite is good at helping with jaw-related issues and dental problems too. It can be a useful adjunct to breathing therapies.

A common mineral, blue calcite is found worldwide. Much of what is sold in the US is native to or mined in Mexico.

GREEN CALCITE

Found in varying shades of green,
this calcite works through the heart
chakra, stabilizing your desires and
encouraging love in all its facets.

E motionally, it helps heal a broken heart. If you keep it nearby to connect with its frequency, it will help you learn to forgive and hopefully forget old wounds and hurts that may haunt your spirit. Green calcite can help balance those feelings, allowing you to open your heart to love once again. Even when you are weighed down with a sense of loss or betrayal, it can help restore a sense of hope and optimism. Green calcite encourages compassion in ourselves and others by clearing away the stagnant and harmful energies that may have accumulated over our lifetime. When used in meditations that are focused on love, it can unlock our hearts and minds to welcome the divine love that surrounds each of us. When we draw upon this type of positive energy, it has a calming influence on our vengeful reflexes, allowing us to grow in understanding and forgiveness.

Like the other colors of calcite, this stone is a good choice for any bone or joint problem where there is an imbalance or lack of calcium. It supports the growth of broken bones by aiding cellular regeneration in their repair. Green calcite is associated with the heart chakra, helping to clear blockages while allowing for the free flow of energy. This action helps repair and restore the heart back to normalcy, especially after surgery. It can be used for most issues that deal with the lungs, heart, and other vital organs in the chest cavity. It is also a good stone to use in healing layouts for arthritis because it helps reduce the inflammation that causes pain.

Like the other calcites, green calcite is a common stone that is found in many locations around the world.

ORANGE CALCITE

This crystal works mainly through the **SACRAL CHAKRA**, though it can be used on any of the first three chakra centers in healing rituals.

Orange calcite is very similar to and sometimes confused with yellow calcite. I believe in going with what my eyes tell me for color, as I have seen deep-yellow calcites sold as orange at different locations, even at the supplier level. The fact is that the properties of both are similar as their colors tend to flow from pale and light to deep and dark. The orange hues add more strength to the vibratory nature of this calcite crystal. Therefore, it is a bit more stimulating to the auric field, especially when it comes to lifting depression, removing fear, and bringing more zest into your life. It is considered an excellent stone to carry for improving business and increasing abundance because of its invigorating influence on your self-confidence. Under its influence you are more likely to get out there in the world, becoming more of a go-getter. This, in turn, opens new doorways to opportunities that can usher in the success you seek. Working through the sacral chakra, orange calcite also enlivens a more playful nature and helps animate your sense of creativity and wonder. It can help you explore new paths and find novel ways to complete your projects.

Physically, this stone supports the endocrine system, the metabolism, and lower digestive tract. It's used in healing layouts for irritable-bowel syndrome (IBS) and constipation. It's also useful for clearing blockages in the second chakra that are related to genital, hormonal, and reproductive issues. Its calcium content makes it an excellent choice for bone or skeletal issues, as well as aiding in the healing of skin or connective-tissue disorders.

Like the rest of the calcite family, this calcium carbonate mineral is found in various places around the world, including North and South America.

YELLOW CALCITE

The frequency of this sunny-
colored crystal is great for lifting
your spirit as well as amplifying
your self-confidence.

Working through the solar plexus chakra, yellow calcite can also be considered a stone of hope. When your outlook is dimmed by circumstances seemingly beyond your control, this calcite restores that sense of optimism and faith that things will get better. When used in meditation, it can bring back your self-esteem, opening your eyes to a wider realm of possibilities, helping you climb out of your doldrums. This renewed sense of belief can help you deal with the real world, making you ready to tackle the issues that depressed you in the first place. Personally, whenever I find myself feeling overwhelmed by the world, I pick one up and wear it for a day or two. It always helps me *see the light*, as it were, and quit my self-fulfilling gloomy outlook. The yellow calcite simply helps you shake off that heavy feeling. I know it has helped me feel that balance has been restored to the world, and I am better able to tackle whatever challenge is confronting me. When placed near the crown chakra during meditations, yellow calcite works toward elevating your soul toward a higher level of consciousness, helping you make a connection with the universal spirit. It increases an inner alertness and awareness of the more expansive reality that surrounds us.

Physically, this stone is very tuned into the stomach and digestive system. By purifying and clearing blockages in this area, it assists the other organs of elimination, such as the kidneys and bladder. It's also useful in relieving muscle aches and pains, as well as helping with hormonal imbalances when used in healing meditations. Many find this calcite also works to alleviate the pain associated with arthritis.

Yellow calcite is found in North America, South America (primarily Brazil and Peru), and parts of Europe.

CARNELIAN

Aligned with the lower three energy
centers, it's generally associated with
the **SACRAL CHAKRA**.

This orange variety of chalcedony gets its color from the inclusion of iron oxides and appears from a very pale orange to a deep, dark shade of rust. When used on the root chakra, the energy of carnelian can help anchor you to this reality. Moving up to the sacral energy center, it is invigorating for your sense of self-worth, creativity, and sexuality. Considered a stone of courage, it gives you the confidence needed to assert yourself, whether it be on the job, at home, or in a social setting. It's a good stone for those who work with the public as it helps you maintain your sense of composure while holding your ground. It can boost your self-esteem and instill courage, making it especially useful for those who normally allow others to subjugate them or treat them poorly. Carnelian is also a great stone to carry or wear on a regular basis for career advancement. It inspires self-confidence when you are attempting to climb the ladder of success or work on projects that will ultimately advance your career goals.

Physically, carnelian is considered a great stone for clearing the bloodstream and aiding many associated disorders such as hemorrhoids, varicose veins, and phlebitis. It is also useful for detoxing in general and can help with sexual or genital disorders when used over the sacral chakra in healings. Those suffering from arthritis, rheumatism, and lower-back pains can also benefit from wearing this crystal. A warming and motivating stone, it restores lost vitality and energy to those who are feeling lethargic. Drinking carnelian water is reported to help with bleeding gums and sagging skin by increasing the circulation, as well as aiding in cellular regeneration after injury or surgery.

Carnelian can be found in many places around the world, including India and Brazil.

CELESTITE

The soothing, pale-blue crystals of this stone are great environmental cleansers, purifying the air and adding positive energy to the surrounding atmosphere.

I n doing so, they allow the stress and tensions of daily life to gently slip away into the ether. Associated with the top three chakras, these crystals are good to use when meditating upon higher-level spiritual realms. It helps you harmonize with the collective union of light and love, restoring your sense of oneness with the Universal Spirit, or God. Celestite is great at clearing the auric field and offering protection from negative forces. It helps open the third-eye chakra, assisting with developing clairvoyance and intuitive abilities. This is an excellent crystal to station near you, on your desk at work or by your bedside at night, to reduce the effects of fear and anxiety. Its calming influence works wonders when you are going through a difficult period. Meditating inside a grid of at least four different crystals can help you achieve a deeper state of contemplation and introspection. It can also help you communicate with the angels or other beings in the higher-level realms.

Physically, celestite can aid you with various throat or speaking issues and other disorders or problems dealing with the eyes, ears, and nose. Celestite is another good choice of crystal to use for relieving tension headaches, especially if amethyst doesn't seem to work for you. It has also been used in healing rituals or layouts to help those suffering from tinnitus as well as sleep apnea. Once again, keep the crystals near your bedside or pillow for the best energetic exchange to occur while you sleep. Avoid setting these stones in sunny windows as they will tend to lose their color in direct sunlight.

Some of the better grades of celestite normally come from Madagascar, but it can also be found in Brazil and China.

CHAROITE

A stone of the purple ray that is linked with the **THIRD-EYE AND CROWN CHAKRAS**, charoite can be used on all the chakras for spiritual cleansing.

C haroite is another one of those stones that sings to the highest level. The strength and purity of its vibrational frequency make it a good protective stone against negative energies and psychic attacks. It was recently discovered, in the middle of the last century in Siberia, and has fascinated crystal healers around the world with its energy. Charoite is a great purification stone for the entire auric field. It works well with layouts from the Earth star to the soul star (the energy points just below the feet to the one just above the head). Many give it credit for aiding inner transformations that allow you to release old habits and fears and open yourself to a more universal awareness of the spirit within. It is through this release of old fears and habits that true inner healing can begin. Charoite can bring more synchronicity into your life, those seemingly coincidental occurrences that can have more apparent meaning than is first realized. These may help you not only seek a better path to follow but also step onto that path and proceed toward a more spiritual existence.

Physically, the healing energy of this crystal focuses on cleansing the spirit body of blockages and negativity that are the cause of physical disorders and disease. When worked with through the crown chakra, it's been found useful in combating mental problems such as bipolar disorder and autism. Charoite helps with general nervous-system disorders such as restless-leg syndrome, as well as relieving cramps and headaches. When placed under your pillow it encourages deep sleep and pleasant dreams, dispels nightmares, and assists in lucid dreaming.

This rare silicate mineral of phosphorous, calcium, and sodium is mined in Russia.

CHRYSOCOLLA

This is a good crystal for any heartfelt, emotionally depressive thoughts or feelings, as it can help heal tears and clear attachments of the auric field.

T he beauty of these stones is their remarkable blend of blues and greens. These colors link chrysocolla with the heart and throat chakra when used in healing meditations and rituals. Tradition states that chrysocolla was the chosen stone for those who lived alone—monks, hermits, or people simply on their own—as it had the ability to give one a calm acceptance of their solitary ways. Conversely, it has the power to enhance your compassion and concern for others when it is carried about on a regular basis. It can lift from your spirit the sadness and grief of a lost love, while opening your heart chakra to life and the ability to forgive past wrongs. Chrysocolla is also considered a stone of positive grounding energy that can be helpful in anchoring your emotional nature and lessening your naivete (not believing everything you hear). While this crystal keeps your eyes and ears open for the truth of matters, you are less likely to react out of hand to challenges in your love life.

Physically, this is a good crystal to wear for stress and anxiety issues, particularly ones related to your love life. Naturally, it is good for most heart-related ailments, as well as cramps, childbirth, and PMS. When worn, it regulates blood pressure and is useful for healings of the lungs and for back pain. When working through the throat chakra, it helps with the adrenal and thyroid glands as well as sore throats. Some people find it helpful with reducing the pain of arthritis and rheumatism.

This greenish-blue crystal, a hydrous copper aluminum silicate, can be found in many places, including Russia, Chile, Africa, and the US.

CHRYSOPRASE

This crystal carries a
compassionate vibration that
is a calming influence on an
overburdened heart.

A s with most green stones, chrysoprase is associated primarily with the heart chakra, where it offers loving peace to those who meditate upon the crystal or carry it with them. It can help you fall into a pleasant sleep mode at night when kept under the pillow or held in your hand. And as a stone of compassion, it lifts the spirit to a level of universal love that brings inner joy to the soul. Chrysoprase can also help ease you into a meditative state when trying to still the mind. Working through the heart, it restores feelings of hopefulness and joy to those who are feeling depressed and lost. It simply generates a sense of grace, security, peace, and love when carried or worn on a regular basis. Lore from the Middle Ages tells us that chrysoprase should be recharged at the half moon to ensure good health and a happy marriage. It was also considered a stone of youth as it strengthened the vitality of those who carried it, invigorating the body as well as the mind. Chrysoprase was not only carried to attract prosperity and good fortune in the past but was used to attract love and marriage too.

This stone tunes into the emotional and physical nature of the heart and is useful in healings that deal with any heart- and lung-related issues, from anxieties and tension that may cause angina, to the balancing of the heart rhythm itself, when worn close to this chakra center. It helps with cellular regeneration, can assist in regulating the hormonal system, and helps balance the metabolism, and the more yellowish stones work well on the stomach and digestive issues.

A silicon dioxide mineral with nickel inclusions, this crystal can be found in Brazil, South Africa, Russia, the US, and Australia.

CITRINE

The joy of this crystal is
obvious in its lemon-yellow
to amber coloring.

Closely associated with the solar plexus chakra, it is also known to work well through the crown and sacral chakras. A great energizing stone, citrine is an excellent cleanser, able to clear the auric field of depressing attachments and other negative energies while bringing a higher light energy to bear.

Wear citrine to increase your self-will and confidence, which in turn will lead you to increase your ability to manifest those things or circumstances you want in life.

Citrine is also useful in protecting you from the negative energies of others as its light energy helps form a dynamic shield around the wearer. It has also been used as a dietary aid, increasing the metabolism to burn calories. Many crystal enthusiasts say it is especially beneficial when used as an elixir and drunk daily for this purpose. Whenever I wear a citrine necklace, I find myself accomplishing a lot more than usual. The energizing effect of this crystal keeps me going when I would normally be stopping for a break or a nap! I must take it off at night or I can't sleep. Personally, I believe citrine vibrates well with my frequency, and that is why it has a strong effect on my being.

In healing layouts, citrine is a good stone that brings balance to the upper digestive tract, as well as acting as a filter for the spleen and pancreas. It can help relieve constipation as it works on clearing the sacral and solar plexus chakras. Citrine is also useful for creative endeavors when used in meditations upon the crown chakra.

A form of quartz, this silicon dioxide mineral ranges in color from light yellow to deeper amber tones. It is mostly found in Brazil, parts of Europe, Madagascar, Russia, and the US.

DUMORTIERITE

The basic blue color of this
stone belies the energy it holds
to help you in many ways.

Associated with the throat chakra, it works just as well when used in meditations that focus on increasing third-eye abilities. It helps develop latent psychic powers such as telepathy, clairaudience, and clairvoyance. For this reason, it is a great stone to wear when you are working with Tarot cards or other means of divination, as it strengthens those intuitive flashes and inner visions that allow you to give a more definitive reading. Dumortierite increases your mental and intellectual capabilities as well. It helps you learn new things, such as when students are studying for a test or people are starting new jobs. It seems to increase your mental alertness, allowing for the retention of new information as well as boosting your memory capabilities.

Dumortierite soothes away inflammatory reactions and emotions that cause us to overreact in anger. This leads the way to a more dispassionate understanding of what is causing our inner turmoil, and allows us to reason out our problems, rather than making them worse because we've lost control. This stone can also be worn or used for its calming influence when we are feeling overstressed and overwhelmed by the daily problems that life throws our way. Simply wearing or holding on to a dumortierite during these times can help restore calm to our spirits.

Physically, this stone is used to quell headaches when kept near the head. Lying down with one crystal on either side of your temples is the best way to achieve this healing. Due to its ability to help clear and strengthen the mind, dumortierite is most often used for emotional or mental problems such as depression, foggy thinking, and confusion due to its ability to help clear and strengthen the mind.

This crystal is an aluminum borate silicate mineral that can be found in many places, including North and South America, Europe, Africa, and Russia.

FLUORITE

The beauty of this crystal is
apparent in its blending of
rainbow colors, which helps
dissolve old habits and harmful
behavioral problems.

It clears the higher chakra levels, aligning them with their Divine Imprint. Through this action, your aura resonates more easily with the spirit body, allowing for inner growth and personal fulfillment. It has a stabilizing effect on the auric field that allows it to block incoming harmful energy. It can boost creativity in the artist and increase psychic awareness and intuition and is used in meditations to help one connect with ethereal beings from higher realms. Fluorite helps balance one's inner and outer consciences, creating a complete and more balanced psyche. Fluorite also has the added benefit of balancing the emotions and stabilizing the thought process to enhance mental clarity and focus. It can reduce stress and anxiety when carried or worn on a habitual basis. Fluorite also works to declutter your mind, making it a great choice for meditation practices.

Physically, fluorite is supportive of the brain, teeth, bones, and skin. It can offer pain relief to those suffering from arthritis and rheumatism. Depending on the color, fluorite works in healings for most areas of the body. You simply associate the colors in this crystal with the parts of the body linked with the seven chakras. For example, fluorites that are mostly yellow or orange in color will work on problems associated with the sacral and solar plexus chakras. Stones that are mostly green in color are well suited to work on heart and lung issues, both physical and emotional. Blue-colored stones are good for any throat-related or thyroid problem, and the purple fluorites are great energy clearers for the entire auric field, removing blockages and dispelling attachments that have grown over time.

Fluorite is a calcium fluoride mineral that is found in the US, China, Europe, and South America.

GREEN FUCHSITE

A form of mica, green fuchsite is normally associated with the **HEART CHAKRA**, though it works well throughout the entire meridian system and auric field.

For this reason, it is often referred to as the healer's stone. It's a great choice for those who perform Reiki and other healing therapies. This shiny crystal has a splendid array of attributes besides its innate healing qualities. The sparkling green color of this crystal is believed to attract and facilitate communication with fairies. Therefore, it is another good choice for those who love the outdoors and gardening. Place a few stones around your garden and see how your plants respond to the loving growth energy this crystal offers. Green fuchsite, when kept close, also has a rejuvenating effect on the mind, restoring a sense of youth, wonder, and hope when kept close. Carry it with you to attract luck and abundance in all the good things life has to offer. Holding on to this crystal will raise your spirits and put a smile on your face as it raises your vibrational frequency to a higher, happier level. Green fuchsite is a great stone to use when stress and tension are getting you down. It helps alleviate those negative emotions and restore a sense of balance with the world around you. It can also be used in concert with other crystals to invigorate and strengthen their own inner power.

Physically, this crystal can help with heart and lung issues, aiding cellular regeneration and healing. It works well for those who wish to alleviate muscle strains and tears, especially those aches and pains in the back and shoulders. It helps calm inflammations and aids those with carpel tunnel syndrome.

This form of muscovite is a potassium silicate aluminum hydroxide fluoride mineral with chromium inclusions that cause the green color. It is most often found in South Africa, India, Russia, and the Alps.

GARNET

There are different types of garnet
that run the gamut from yellows and
greens to dark reds and browns.

W e will be describing a specific type known as almandine garnet, the one we feel is more familiar and more commonly found in crystal-and-stone shops. This deep-red crystal works primarily through the root chakra, grounding and sustaining your physical endurance with the natural Earth energy. Garnet is a strong regenerative stone for both the spiritual and physical bodies. It has a vital restorative force on the body, increasing stamina and drive. It's used in meditations to raise the kundalini energy up through the chakra system, which is helpful for those who are prepared to grow their spiritual connections to a higher level of awareness. It's also considered a good stone for psychic protection. It has the strength to deflect negative energies from attaching themselves to a person, repelling their hold over the wearer. For this reason, it has historically been worn or carried for protection and courage in the face of battle. Another facet of this dark crystal is that traditionally it has been believed to attract love into your life when worn on a regular basis, the lighter colors having more of this energy than the darker ones, as they work more through the heart chakra than the root.

Physically, garnet is a good stone to use in healings of the reproductive system, as well as to help in general recovery from surgery and injuries. It also helps restore balance to issues arising in the lower digestive tract. Garnet is a useful stone for spinal disorders and pain. It is stimulating to the metabolism and can help regenerate and repair DNA.

An iron aluminum silicate crystal, garnet can be found in Alaska, Arizona, Brazil, Sri Lanka, India, and other places around the world, depending on the type.

GOLDSTONE

Though technically not a crystal, this copper-infused wonder was created back in the seventeenth century by the Miotti family in Venice, Italy.

G oldstone is, therefore, man-made and created by melting silica (ground quartz or quartz sand), chemicals, and copper salts that return to their metallic state during the processing. The copper coloring of this crystal falls between the orange and red spectrum, synchronizing its vibratory rate with the first two chakra centers, the root and sacral. It's useful for energizing these areas of the auric field and is listed and sold as a healing crystal due to the vibrational energy of the copper when fused inside the quartz glass.

Goldstone can raise your verve and vitality while adding an energetic bounce to your nature. Working through the sacral chakra, it opens the doorway to inner creativity and inspiration. The metal copper has traditionally been used in healing throughout the years. It has been worn in bracelets to alleviate the pain of arthritis and rheumatism. It's a great choice when you want to heal the aura in general because it balances the polarity of the entire energetic field. It can enhance the therapeutic frequencies sent by those in the healing professions, encouraging the vital energy streams between the practitioner/sender and the receiver. Another quality of the metal copper is its relationship to the planet Venus. Traditionally, it was considered to be lucky and able to attract a loving mate. This artificial crystal can also be used as a stone of protection for its ability to deflect negative energies. Carrying a goldstone or wearing the jewelry can help protect the spirit from unwanted attachments and thwart harmful vibrations.

Physically, goldstone has been used to stimulate the flow of energy, increasing your natural strength and stamina. It helps with inflammatory conditions such as arthritis and joint pain, as well as stabilizing the metabolism and nervous system.

HEMATITE

This metallic-looking gray stone
is well known for its grounding
and protective qualities.

L inked with the root chakra, hematite is the premier choice to wear when grounding yourself to the realities of life. It can help those who find their head in the clouds much of the time, to face the facts of daily life in a rational manner. It can also assist you when you are trying to bring your dreams to fruition by helping you figure out the best possible way in which to achieve the desired result. Of course, this usually entails knuckling down and getting to work, doing what needs to be done in a methodical way to achieve your goals. When used in meditations, hematite can help you keep your sense of identity amid more-spiritual realms where dreams can become reality. In this way, it acts as protection against losing yourself in a myriad of possibilities and helps you focus on pertinent goals. It's also a highly recommended stone used by many when they are concerned about ghostly attachments and attacks. Hematite has a reputation for repelling negative energies and unwanted vibes from entering your auric field, especially if you are ghost hunting or simply trying to connect with the other side. Too often, people try contacting whatever spirit might be inhabiting a location without knowing whether it is good or evil. That's when wearing a hematite comes into play, protecting the auric field and repelling unwanted intrusions into the spirit.

Due to its iron component, hematite is known to support the circulatory system and help with diseases of the bloodstream. It also helps with insomnia by calming down widely scattered thoughts that plague you at night.

Hematite is an iron oxide mineral that can be found in many places, including North and South America, northern Europe, and, most recently, Australia.

HOWLITE

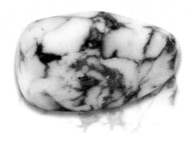

Appearing like a small piece of
marble, this stone is often artificially
colored to look like turquoise.

Being basically white, it is usually linked to the crown chakra; however, it works as well on the entire chakra system when used in healing layouts. When used in meditations, place it over the third-eye chakra to help open and allow yourself to sink deeper into that alpha state. From there, you can relax and focus on deepening your practice even further, allowing you to explore the higher realms of spiritual attunement and the vast openness of ethereal space. Holding on to a howlite at this juncture can help access past lives and the lessons learned from them. By letting go of mistakes and pains from the past, we begin to heal our spirit and body in the here and now. This in turn can help us in our progress toward a more loving and spiritual life in our present incarnation. A peaceful stone, howlite is great for calming the spirit and releasing stress and tension that is held in the back and shoulders. This stone is also an excellent choice for those who simply want to slow down and smell the roses as they travel through life. Wear it daily as a reminder that the beauty of life is in the simple things, and a carefree life starts with the removal of guilt, greed, and the myriad of stresses we tend to hold within. Howlite can help us move past all these emotions and simply be who we are, and learn to accept others as they are.

When placed under your pillow, howlite can help you get a good night's rest. It helps to balance calcium levels in the body and is useful in healings for the bones and teeth.

A calcium silicate-borate mineral, this stone was discovered and is mainly mined in Canada.

NEPHRITE JADE

Nephrite jade is most often found
in crystal-and-stone shops and is
like true jade because they share
similar vibrational patterns.

Nephrite's dark-green color is associated with the heart chakra. As with other green stones, nephrite jade is believed to bring good luck to the wearer, inviting wealth and prosperity into your life. It is a good choice to use in meditations and layouts when you are clearing your auric field because it sweeps away those depressive and negative energies that may linger there. It helps restore a sense of well-being and can bring joy back into your life when carried on a regular basis. It offers emotional healing to those who are grieving or broken hearted and can help lift their spirits from the depths of despair. The strength it imparts to you when wearing it can restore a sense of harmony and balance to your life, especially when you are at odds with others in your community. The ability of jade to open and clear the heart chakra brings you to a wider understanding of those who oppose you, and it helps find a way to cooperate with others on a more even keel. It imparts a sense of purity and love to the emotions, so you can reach a place of serenity in spirit. Sleeping with this stone under your pillow can help bring about pleasant dreams that can be inspiring.

Jade is a good choice to use in healing layouts or simply to wear every day when your healing needs are related to the heart, lungs, liver, and kidneys, as it helps those organs filter out toxins and stabilize themselves. It adds vitality and can invigorate the immune system, which in turn is supportive of your overall general health.

Nephrite jade is a calcium, magnesium, and iron silicate that can be found in many places, including North America, Russia, and China.

JASPER

All jaspers share the qualities of
strength, courage, and stability.

J aspers come in so many variations from all around the world that an entire book could be written on them alone. The main color of each style should be used to associate it with its sympathetic chakra center. Their energy is more of a slow, steady infusion, but when worn on a regular basis, they can be very effective over the long term. Marketing mavens around the world have given distinctive names to most of the patterns and colors that have been discovered, such as leopard, turtle, snake, dalmatian, and so on. There appears to be a name for every single pattern, and many of these are very similar in appearance. The most important thing to remember is that they will associate with their corresponding chakra color. Some of these stones have previously been listed under the "Crystals by Color" sections earlier in the book. For the sake of brevity, I will list a few of the more common jaspers that are easily obtainable along with a brief description of each.

BRECCIATED JASPER

It is felt to be a very good
grounding and protective stone.

This jasper is formed from the inclusion of hematite and chalcedony. It can assist with tamping down sexually aggressive tendencies, helping you maintain more self-control. Working through the first and second chakras, it aids with issues related to the circulation as well as the regeneration of tissue. It can help you with a return to normalcy following a lengthy illness. It is a good stone for detoxification of the internal organs of elimination, as well as being very useful in cleansing the entire auric field of negative energies.

LEOPARD JASPER

This stone is yet another variety that is good for those who work with animals.

It is also recommended for those who take shamanic journeys, helping them connect with their animal spirit or totem. It comes in many colors from reds and greens to tans and browns, with a unique spotted pattern. Leopard jasper is recommended to carry when you need to work closely with others as it helps people understand and get along with each other. It works on the lower three chakras in healing rituals, depending on the color, and helps with detoxification and eliminations.

PICTURE JASPER

The striations on this gold or creamy tan-colored jasper can beautifully show its association with the Earth.

These stones are believed to resonate with ley lines and places of power and are used to increase your own inner strength and personal power. They are often used in dream work and focused meditations when you are looking to journey within and discover your own psychological or spiritual landscape. Picture jasper can imbue you with a sense of security and structure. Physically, it is an aid in the healing of the skeletal structure and can help calm muscle spasms.

RED JASPER

Red Jasper is a great energizer, one that gives strength to the spirit as well as the body.

It helps with organizational abilities and determination. Historically, it was carried by warriors to increase their courage and protect them on the battlefield. In meditations it is used to balance and cleanse the auric field and increase the protective strength of your etheric shield, keeping out negative energies and attachments. This crystal is often used in healings that concern the lower digestive tract, kidneys, hemorrhoids, and gout. It is helpful for the regeneration of muscle tissue and recovery after illness.

UNIKITE JASPER

This green stone with orange flecks aligns with the **HEART CHAKRA**, though it can be used for healings on all the chakra centers.

Unikite promotes a healthful level of compassion for others and encourages mutual respect and growth in relationships. It can be worn to help overcome addictive patterns of behavior such as smoking. It aids the body in the regeneration of healthy tissue and can offer the spiritual and physical support needed for cancer and other serious illnesses. It is believed to help align the various spiritual bodies with the physical body when worn over time.

JET

This stone is well known
for its ability to clear and
purify the auric field.

B y cleansing away the negative energies, it encourages healing on a spiritual level. A black stone that works through the first root chakra, jet is a great choice for grounding you in the present reality. That is why it is useful for those who are given to flights of fancy, or daydreaming, helping them focus on the job at hand. With a jet stone in your pocket, it is easier to apply yourself and concentrate on whatever project you are working on. It's also a great stone to use as protection from negative forces or attachments. It strengthens the spiritual body, deflecting any harmful vibrations that are directed toward it. It can be used as a cleansing crystal, like hematite. Simply put the crystal or stone you need to cleanse in a bowl that has several pieces of jet inside, and let it sit for several hours. It will clear and purify them of harmful vibrations and attachments. Jet is another stone that is often worn by active ghost hunters to anchor and protect their spirits when attempting communication with departed souls or when trying to cleanse a house or space of negative entities or vibrations. It has also been useful for those who are focusing themselves on finding their inner magic, helping to release this latent power they feel within.

This stone tends to work more on the etheric level, through the meridian system, by energizing your body's own natural healing abilities. It is recommended for the energetic treatment of head and nerve issues such as headaches and epilepsy. It has also been found useful in calming some forms of anxiety and in cleansing the lower-body organs of elimination.

This stone is a form of coal that can be found in many places, including Europe, Russia, Australia, and the US.

BLUE KYANITE

When used in meditations, it's great for
stimulating the **THIRD-EYE CHAKRA**,
enhancing your ability to perceive
information from higher sources, and
increasing psychic awareness.

T he shiny, bladelike structure of this blue crystal can be fascinating to behold. It helps awaken you to the interdimensional worlds when practicing deeper meditations. This stone can also improve your communication with higher-dimensional beings. Sleeping with a blade of blue kyanite under your pillow can improve your dream recall and encourage vivid and lucid dreaming.

This crystal is believed to bridge energy gaps in the body from traumas and surgeries and is used to aid victims of strokes and seizures by helping create new neural pathways around damaged ones. Working through the crown chakra, it helps those with nervous disorders as well as headaches. The fast frequency of kyanite raises its vibrational rate, which allows for quicker energy transfers that can help speed up the healing process. It works well on the entire chakra system and is especially good for problems stemming from the throat area, such as laryngitis. Teachers, salespeople, and others who benefit from using their influence through the spoken word would be well advised to carry this stone in their pocket throughout the day. Blue kyanite is recommended for those with muscular problems and in need of general pain relief. It is also used in healing layouts to treat the adrenal and thyroid glands.

Kyanite is an aluminum silicate mineral that comes in several colors, including black, green, pink, and orange. This stone is reputed not to need cleansing as it does not hold on to negative energy; however, you may want to recharge it occasionally on a sunny windowsill or in the moonlight. Avoid water or saltwater cleansing to protect the stone from degrading. It can be found in North and South America as well as Africa and Burma.

LABRADORITE

It works well on all the **CHAKRA CENTERS** of the body, especially the crown and third eye, as it activates and encourages mental expansion.

I ridescent flashes of color on the surface of this crystal glimmer, giving it a magical appearance that can be deeply fascinating. This makes it a very good choice for those who wish to expand their psychic sense, increase their intuition, and open their inner vision through meditative practices. It encourages clairvoyance and is a useful stone to wear when performing divinations. Labradorite can also assist you when attempting astral travel, helping protect your spirit when it enters the ethereal spheres of reality. Mystical in appearance, it can also be an aid to those who wish to work a little magic, helping them in finding their inner power and ability to manifest their desires. It seems to increase synchronicity in life and can be used to awaken a latent ability to communicate with spirit guides and the angelic realms if you have that true desire within.

When used in healing rituals and meditations, labradorite can increase the effects of other stones and amplify the power of prayers and affirmations for the person being healed. It can help with disorders of the brain and eyes. It is also useful in detoxifying the system from the effects of various addictions. It supports the metabolism through the glandular system, and some have used it for the treatment of arthritis, rheumatism, and gout. Working through the crown chakra, it helps those with problems and disorders affecting the nerves and brain, as well as being used in healings for eye problems. It can help lower the blood pressure and relieve stress when carried about on a regular basis.

This stone is a calcium sodium aluminum silicate mineral that is a member of the feldspar family and is normally found in Canada, North America, and Madagascar.

LAPIS LAZULI

Another sparkling stone of the blue spectrum, lapis lazuli is most often associated with the **THROAT CHAKRA** but works just as well on the third-eye center.

This special gem has many applications depending on the individual who carries or wears it. It may be too strong for some to utilize daily, in which case it's best used in healing layouts and clearings. It's good for opening the third eye, improving natural intuition, and increasing psychic awareness. It can aid you in meditations to send your spirit into the ether to travel through the astral spheres. Lapis lazuli increases your mental faculties and allows you to focus and concentrate. It can help with self-confidence through its ability to let a person simply "know" they are right when they are. Or, conversely, it leads them to the realization that perhaps they haven't seen all the facts. It's a good meditation stone that can help you stay attentive and tune into the creative universe, feeling the at-one-ness of the material and spiritual realms. It strengthens the auric field and clears away harmful energies, making it perfect for chakra cleansings and healing rituals.

Lapis can be useful as a pain reliever, mitigating migraines and headaches as well as helping those dealing with chronic aches and pains in various parts of the body. When seeking a peaceful night's rest, lapis helps you relax and drift into dreamland. It's also recommended to assist with balance issues brought about by vertigo. It gives vitality and strength to the body when it is run down, and is considered helpful in clarifying the truth in situations where previously conditions seemed clouded. It's useful for healing most any situation or condition pertaining to the head and throat area.

Lapis lazuli is a sodium aluminum silicate that comes from many places, including Afghanistan, the US, Russia, and the Middle East.

LEPIDOLITE

A stone of the mica group,
purple lepidolite twinkles when
seen in the light and is perfect
for **WORKING ON ALL THE
CHAKRAS**, especially the third eye.

Its higher vibrational frequency is used to open the third eye, awaken the inner psychic senses, and promote an awareness of the more ethereal realms of existence. For this reason, it's considered optimal for deepening meditative states. Lepidolite is simply a great option to use when quieting the mind. It instills a calmness to the emotions that allows you to relax inside. Personally, I wear a lepidolite necklace whenever I find myself in that scatterbrained mode on busy days. It helps me to stop running around in circles and to focus on the task at hand without worrying about what needs to be done next! It's also useful when worn to alleviate depression and despondency as it clears away the negativity that has attached itself to the auric field. This makes it a grand stone to wear when feeling anxious and stressed out, since it clears away all those harmful vibrations that feed our anxieties. Lepidolite is also one of the better stone choices for filtering or blocking the electromagnetic vibrations that emanate from computers and other modern equipment. Simply keep it nearby or place it on the offending machine itself.

Physically, it is utilized for many disorders of the mind, such as Alzheimer's, ADD and ADHD, schizophrenia, bipolar disease, and the like. It has been carried to aid those with muscular skeletal problems, arthritis, and rheumatism, as well as various allergies. It can be helpful in preventing nightmares and insomnia as it induces a calming influence on the mind. It can be used in healings along the entire meridian system to clear the chakras of blockages and attachments.

Lepidolite is a potassium lithium aluminum silicate mineral that generally is found in Greenland, North and South America, and Africa.

MALACHITE

Associated with the **HEART AND SACRAL CHAKRAS**, it works well on emotional and physical issues that are centered here.

The distinctive swirly pattern on this green stone attracts your attention. Being a stone that resonates with the heart center, malachite can help you build a more profound sense of compassion and empathy toward others. During meditations it can also be placed over the third eye to increase psychic intuitions and enlighten the spirit so that it may grow in peace and harmony. When worn on a regular basis, it can help you attain a state of emotional harmony and stability. Malachite is also used to feel a connection to the natural world surrounding us and is another stone that can help you connect with the devic realms of nature. Malachite is excellent at clearing an area of radiation and electromagnetic pollutants and is one of the best stones to keep on your electronic equipment such as computers and printers, especially when you work with these machines every day.

This stone can be used in healing grids and layouts for female reproductive disorders, as well as relieving the pain of menstrual cramps when kept in your pocket near the lower abdomen. Many find it helps relieve the aches and pain of arthritis and rheumatism through its anti-inflammatory emanations. Naturally, it works well with any heart-related issues as well as strengthening the immune system. Malachite can help heal health problems with the lungs, liver, kidneys, and the muscular/skeletal system when used in healing therapies such as Reiki. Be advised, though, that the chemical composition of malachite is best if only used in its polished form. Never use it in an elixir and avoid breathing in its dust if you possess it in raw form.

This green stone is a copper carbonate that can be found in Africa, Russia, and North and South America, as well as Australia.

MICA

Mica is one of those crystals that works on a more etheric level, cleansing the auric field and clearing it of attachments and harmful blockages.

There are several groups of crystals that are close chemical relatives of mica, each having their own unique qualities. Lepidolite, fuchsite, and kyanite are some of the associated forms of mica. The distinctive layers and pearl-like coloring, along with an aluminum-like reflective surface, give mica its unique appearance. The nature of this crystal works well on all the chakra centers.

Mica helps deflect negative energies, keeping them at bay. Therefore, it is a good crystal to sit on your desk at work or near your bed at night to encourage a more harmonious atmosphere. Working through the crown chakra, mica helps on a mental level, calming anxiety attacks and balancing your emotional state. When used in meditations, it becomes a stone of transformation as it accelerates your spiritual growth and understanding. It helps those who are seeking a higher wisdom to open their minds and hearts to the universal knowledge. It helps you improve your natural intuition and expand your psychic abilities. Mica can increase the chance of synchronicity in your life, acting as a sort of guidepost, either backing up your convictions or pointing out where you are going wrong. It also helps when are trying to change your direction, by helping you let go of old attachments and habits while finding the inner strength to move forward in your life. As a balancing crystal, mica helps with nervous habits and ticks as well as leveling out the extra energies linked to those with ADHD. It can help you with memory and concentration, as well as supporting strength and stamina in the physical body.

A potassium aluminum silicate, mica can be found in areas of North and South America, Russia, Africa, and India.

MOLDAVITE

Moldavite is a form of tektite and is
believed to have been created millions
of years ago when meteorites were
striking the Earth, and for this reason
it is considered to have a partially
extraterrestrial origin.

True moldavite only comes from the Czech Republic and is mostly green in color. Other tektites formed from meteorite collisions are scattered around the world. Moldavite is believed to be of a higher vibrational frequency and therefore is the prime choice to open and clear all the chakras, from the root to the crown, bringing them into alignment with the universal source of life.

This glassy stone is very good when used to open the third eye. Placing it there in meditations helps increase awareness of the higher ethereal realms and creates a portal for those who are truly focused. It's the go-to stone when attempting to instigate communications with extraterrestrials. Considered a stone of transformation and change, it instills the spirit with an inner desire to enlighten and purify oneself, bringing about spiritual and physical changes for the better. The energetic field of moldavite is strong and can easily be felt by many who hold it for the first time. Its ability to open the chakras in meditation is sometimes more intense than with other stones, and, therefore, caution is advised when first working with it so as not to overwhelm yourself with the powerful rush of emotions that can surface under intensive focus.

Physically, moldavite is used to cleanse the entire auric field to help the body naturally heal from any disorder or disease affecting it. Its green coloring gives it a stronger link to the heart chakra, where it helps various heart and lung issues when used in healing rituals or meditations.

This mixture of aluminum silicon or other metal oxides is a form of tektite that was mainly discovered in the Czech Republic.

MOONSTONE

As with the moon itself, these crystals possess a shimmering, light-reflective surface that appeals to our sense of imagination and wonder.

T hey are generally linked to the crown and third-eye chakras for their ability to bring out our intuitive ability and in growing our empathetic natures. When used in meditations they can facilitate delving into the hidden sides of our psyche, digging out what the subconscious has buried and bringing it to light for our conscience exploration and understanding. When worn on a regular basis, they add to synchronicity in life, opening our eyes to patterns we previously overlooked and helping us see matters from a different angle. Being a receptive crystal, moonstone has been worn in the past to draw love into one's life. Focus on the person of your heart's desire while holding the stone, then wear it or keep it close to your body to help draw that person into your life. The moonstone's connection with our lunar disc also makes it a good stone to slip under your pillow at night. By adding a sense of comfort and security, it helps ensure a restful sleep, and when meditated upon it can increase prophetic and lucid dreams. Because of this crystal's association with the feminine side of life, it's attuned to the female reproductive organs and cycles, aiding and stabilizing them. Moonstones help ease cramps and other symptoms of PMS. They also help balance the bodily fluids and the digestive system, particularly the stomach. Moonstones are good crystals for women who are pregnant as they assist in stabilizing the hormones. They soften tensions and calm the nervous system, making them a good choice for calming emotional stress.

A potassium feldspar mineral found in India, Sri Lanka, the Americas, and the Arabian Peninsula, moonstones come in a variety of colors from milky whites, creams, and peachy shades to silvery blacks and browns.

RAINBOW MOONSTONE

This crystal is technically a white labradorite. It carries many similar traits to moonstone and works through the **CROWN, THIRD-EYE, AND THROAT CHAKRAS.**

Many ghost hunters who frequent our shop will carry black obsidian when on ghost tours to keep the spirits of Civil War soldiers from attaching to them. The other side of the coin is that black obsidian has been used for centuries as a scrying tool. The ancient Aztecs polished and used it for divination purposes. The solid, shiny black surface allowed them to focus on clearing their minds and bringing about a heightened state of sensitivity to messages from the spirit world. I would advise a warning for those who are already sensitive to spirits. Because it helps facilitate a connection with the souls of those who have passed, you may find it alarming when opening that doorway. My niece avoids it now because once she wore a black obsidian necklace to bed and woke up with bad dreams that included a Confederate soldier and deceased family member. She said she couldn't remember what was happening, only that she awoke very angry and upset. When realizing she had forgotten to take off the necklace, she slipped it off and put it away. My niece is one of those who rarely remembers dreams. This instance was enough for her; she'll never wear an obsidian again. This is a perfect example of choosing the right stone, and if you find that it isn't working for you, give it away!

This stone is normally associated with the root chakra in healings. As a healing stone, it is more useful in finding the root cause of disorders or diseases affecting you, by clearing the blockages in the aura that impede self-healing.

Black obsidian is a silicon dioxide form of glassy volcanic rock that can be found in volcanic lands, including India, Greece, Mexico, and China.

ONYX

This is an interesting stone because in the past, onyx has been considered an evil or bad luck stone in ancient China, while in the Middle East, it was considered a protective and healing stone, even useful to women during childbirth and lucky for those in business.

Today it is generally associated with being a stone of protection, and one that can be lucky for those who feel a natural connection to it. Though black is the color we commonly associate with onyx, it can be found in various colors, including white, blue, and even shades of gray, brown, and yellow. We are describing the qualities of the black stone here, and that color is linked with the root chakra.

Onyx makes a good grounding stone and one that can help stabilize a situation. It increases your stability and endurance when needed to do brute tasks. It helps develop inner strength, both mentally and physically, by narrowing your focus on your current dealings. In this way it supports your energy, which in turn allows you to accomplish your goals without draining your reserves. Onyx also helps you release anxieties and nervousness, bringing peace to your spirit and a calmness to your mind, especially when life seems to be roiling about you. It is considered a stone of steadiness for its ability to level the etheric playing field, balancing the yin and yang of our energy flows and bringing together conflicting emotions and balancing them. It has been carried to instill a stronger sense of willpower, helping you take charge of situations and stand your ground.

Physically, it helps repair the nervous system and can assist in restoring vitality and strength. It has also been used in healing layouts for bone problems.

Black onyx is a banded form of chalcedony that can be found in North and South America, India, Russia, and parts of Europe.

PINK OPAL

Common opals are found in many colors, including blue, black, violet, orange, and, of course, the semiprecious white opal that is used in most jewelry settings.

We are dealing here with the pink opal, and like the other common opals, it doesn't possess that fiery iridescent appearance of the white opal. However, it does carry its own distinct characteristics that make it special. This crystal opens the heart to divine love and understanding, allowing you to reconnect with your spiritual source. This pink opal can bring peace and joy back into your life, especially if you had previously felt lost or abandoned. It restores a sense of spiritual renewal and inner growth. Working through the heart chakra, it's a calming stone, helping relieve stress and tension when held or worn. Considered a crystal of higher vibrations, pink opal is useful in meditations when seeking to find the cause or meaning of emotional sadness and suffering. It helps you release those old heartaches and pain and revive a sense of hope and joy. It's great when learning to let go of those toxic mindsets, whether they be addictive behaviors, self-destructive emotions, or self-demeaning thought patterns.

Physically these stones are good for issues related to the heart and lungs, liver, and spleen. Wear this stone on a regular basis to allow its healing influence to work on the heart chakra, clearing and cleansing the blockages there. Doing so helps the physical body restore itself to normalcy.

Be mindful not to cleanse this stone in sunlight, as the direct rays of the sun over time will cause it to become brittle and more easily prone to cracking or breaking. It's better to set your crystal under moonlight or cleanse with running water.

Pink opal is a hydrated silica, which is a form of quartz with watery inclusions. It's mostly found in South America, Africa, and Australia.

PREHNITE

This clear green stone has a very loving and soothing vibration, calming your nerves and releasing anxieties that clutter your mind and seem to take hold in your chest.

A s with most green stones, it's connected primarily with the heart chakra; however, those with a yellow tinge can also be effective for use on the solar plexus. It's a great help for those whose nerves feel frayed and who may have developed nervous habits or tics. By aligning the emotional strength of the heart with the inner willpower, it creates a bridge to self-confidence and assurance. In turn, this can bring an inner security of spirit that will alleviate your physical manifestations of nervous tension. With this crystal in hand, prayerful meditations can be increased in strength as it aids in communication with the higher or angelic realms of existence. This is particularly true when the prehnite contains epidote, which naturally increases the power of the energetic frequencies coming from this crystal. Many have carried prehnite when trying to make contact with fairies and other beings of the devic realms. A good multipurpose stone, it can be used as a stone of understanding because it helps you accept the ways of others that differ from your point of view. It does this by opening your heart chakra and inspiring an empathetic spirit and feeling of universal love.

When used in healing, the more yellowish prehnite helps support the digestive system, especially the stomach. Crystals that are more green or blue-green are good for the lungs, heart, and kidneys. It helps balance the circulatory and lymphatic systems and can be used to assist the metabolic processes, which in turn helps with weight control and dieting.

Prehnite is a calcium aluminum silicate mineral, sometimes with epidote inclusions (the black shards pictured) that can be found in South Africa, China, Australia, and the US.

PYRITE

This metallic stone is also
known as fool's gold because of
its similarity to the real thing.

Though lighter in color, it was sometimes used in the past to salt mines in an effort to swindle the inexperienced and hopeful prospector. Conversely, it is now considered a lucky stone and one that when carried can help attract prosperity into your life. It is normally associated with the solar plexus chakra due to its gold coloring.

This stone gives an assertive influence and can help those who need a little kick to get them going. It can build self-confidence and give strength when you are feeling sluggish or lackadaisical. That extra energy promotes ambition and can help you accomplish those boring tasks or, on a larger scale, assist you in reaching your goals in life. Pyrite also gives mental clarity, a helpful trait when attempting to see through a maze of confusing or obfuscating facts. It strengthens your cognitive abilities and memories, aiding you in mental tasks, and is a good choice for those who work in the scientific fields. It can be helpful for students as well by instilling the discipline needed to study lessons after class. Pyrite is also considered a protective stone, deflecting negative energies and environmental pollutants, especially from computers and other electronic devices. When used in clearings it helps repair tears in the auric field.

In healings, pyrite is used to stimulate the digestive process, aid the intestines, and support the liver. Some consider it a helpful stone to carry when fighting viruses or viral infections. This crystal is another one of those that should not be made into an elixir as it can be poisonous due to the breakdown of its mineral content. It is, however, safe to carry or wear.

This iron sulfide mineral is generally found throughout the world, including North and South America, India, and Europe.

CLEAR QUARTZ

This natural wonder
has been called the
mother of all crystals.

Quartz is truly a master crystal for its abilities to be used not only at the crown chakra, but on all chakra centers. Quartz is piezoelectric, meaning it can hold an electrical charge. This quality makes it one of the most versatile stones in the mineral realm. It's used in many products from wrist watches to computers and even kitchen countertops.

You can easily program this crystal by holding it in your hand while mentally focusing your intentions into it. If you need it for stress release, think calming thoughts while staring at it, and it will absorb that energy to aid you in times of need. Then, when you are feeling stressed, simply hold it to release those soothing vibrational frequencies back into your auric field. Quartz is also great if you want to clear blockages from any or all of your chakras. Place it over the chakra you want to clear and mentally see it drawing out any dark or harmful energy you feel. Clearly envision them dissipating into the universe, away from your own auric field. It can also be used in any healing by concentrating on cleansing the ailment from your system during meditations. Simply hold the crystal while sending healing affirmations to that part of your body in need.

Another attribute of quartz is its ability to amplify your psychic impressions and increase your own inner healing powers. It's this amplification property of quartz that makes it such a universally powerful stone and a great "starter" crystal for those just beginning to learn about the stones and crystals.

Quartz comes in a variety of types and forms, such as aqua aura, lemurian seed crystals, phantom quartz, smoky quartz, rutilated quartz, tourmaline quartz, and other variations.

A form of pure silicon dioxide, it's found in locations around the world.

ROSE QUARTZ

Rose quartz has always been linked to the **HEART CHAKRA** as it emanates feelings of love and compassion in their pure form.

I t has a comforting effect on the body and soul, and its soothing vibrations lower stress and anxiety in children as well as adults. Not only does it work on clearing and calming the heart chakra, but it can impart this quality on all the chakra centers. A great choice for healing broken hearts, rose quartz helps with recovery after losing a loved one. By gently allaying our grief and opening our hearts to the preponderance of love the universe has to offer, we begin the healing process. For this reason, it is suggested to wear or carry one daily after suffering such a loss. Rose quartz will restore our sense of emotional security and hope for the future. Sleeping with the stone placed under your pillow or held in your hand can also help those in need of a soothing night's rest. It's also recommended to help soothe and calm restless children.

This form of quartz also assists you in letting go of jealousy and anger. It has a reassuring effect on the heart chakra that allows you to take a breath and release those negative emotions. After an argument with your mate, place a piece of rose quartz under both pillows to nurture a reconciliation. Historically, this crystal was used to attract love into a young maiden's life. It was also carried to invigorate a fading romance.

Physically, rose quartz helps the heart recover from various traumas and disorders when used in healings. It helps remove stress and anxiety, which can lead to a more regular heartbeat.

This pink shade of quartz is a silicon dioxide mineral with inclusions of iron or titanium that cause its coloring. It's found in many places around the world, including Brazil, Madagascar, North America, Austria, and Russia.

RUTILATED QUARTZ

The rutiles found in this type
of quartz are a form of titanium
dioxide that grows in needlelike
shapes inside the crystal.

The blending of these two energies produces a strong capability of amplification, making rutilated quartz an intense crystal to work with. That's why when you are looking to cleanse or purify your chakras, this crystal is the perfect choice for its strength and powerful ability to clear away harmful vibrations and speed up the healing within your auric field. As with the other forms of quartz, it works well with all the chakras, including those above and below the physical body.

Easy to program, rutilated quartz will take the energy you put into it and amplify it to bring about your desired condition. Whether you are using this crystal in a healing layout or magical ritual, as when using it to draw something to you such as prosperity, joy, love, or general health, it will broadcast your desire into the ether, helping bring about the manifestation of your goal. Meditations with this crystal are more intense and help bring you to a higher level of awareness. Rutilated quartz also imparts a sense of peace, serenity, and happiness when impressed with positive thoughts. Simply holding on to a rutilated quartz can bring about a feeling of well-being and inner strength as it fortifies your spirit with its higher frequency.

A great general-healing crystal, this stone is useful in supporting the body's own immune system by helping the physical body repair itself. It has been used for ailments and diseases as diverse as cognitive failure to phantom pain. It appears to work best on crown-related disorders associated with the brain and nerve functions.

Rutilated quartz is a silicon dioxide mineral with inclusions of rutile, and it is mined primarily in Brazil and Madagascar but can also be found in India and Australia.

SMOKY QUARTZ

Smoky quartz derives its color from the free silicon inside the crystal, which has been naturally irradiated over the millennia.

It's considered a very good protection stone for its ability to deflect and transmute the negative vibrational frequencies that may come in contact with your auric field. The brown tint of color in this clear crystal lends itself to an association with the root chakra, and this helps stabilize your entire body-spirit connection. That is why smoky quartz is a great choice for grounding yourself, especially if you tend to flights of fancy. It is also a premier choice for many who want to clear harmful or destructive energies from their entire meridian system. A good way to do this is to stand outside and hold a smoky quartz crystal in each hand. Close your eyes and visualize all the negative accumulations being pulled from your body and sent into the ground. Feel yourself simply letting go while all the harmful forces drain out of your body. It clears the auric field as it washes the damaging energies from you, sending them back into the earth for purification and cleansing. It is a truly remarkable decontamination stone. Another aspect of this crystal has been to use it to when attempting to see or make contact with ghosts, fairies, and elementals from other realms of existence. Being a quartz, it can be easily programmed to assist you in these endeavors by amplifying your psychic messages and sending them through the ethereal realms.

Physically, smoky quartz is recommended for lower-back pain, issues related to the colon and the hips. It has also been used to dissipate muscular cramps and pain. This crystal is believed to help remove toxic accumulations and has been used in healings to lessen the harmful effects of radiation and chemotherapy. It's a silicon dioxide mineral that can be found worldwide.

TOURMALINE QUARTZ

This blended form of quartz
contains strands of black tourmaline
inclusions, making it extra special as
it has the ability to cleanse itself.

One of the more precious crystals, ruby works through the root chakra. It stimulates courage and passion, helping you stand up for what you believe in, thereby building self-confidence. Ruby is also a good choice to use when fighting lethargic impulses and feelings of weakness. When you are about to give up hope because the world has gotten you down, then ruby is the stone you need in your pocket. It can usher in a feeling of renewed hope and restore that necessary drive to accomplish your aims in life. The pure red energy of this crystal can also tune into and work well when you focus your intentions through the heart chakra, bringing love and compassion back into your life. It can revive faded passions and romantic inclinations by opening and clearing the heart chakra of blockages and repairing tears in the auric field. These actions clear the way and welcome more amorous opportunities to occur. Ruby can be considered a lucky stone because it is also used to attract wealth and prosperity when carried regularly on your person.

Working through the lower chakras, ruby is good for helping with problems located in the reproductive organs, spleen, and adrenal glands. It's used to stimulate a sluggish circulation and strengthen the heart; however, it is also known to increase blood pressure and should be avoided by those who already have high blood pressure. It can be used to bolster most of the bodily systems as it fortifies and strengthens the meridians running through the etheric body.

This crystal is a variety of corundum, which is an aluminum oxide mineral. It comes in varying shades of red and is found around the world in such places as Sri Lanka, Southeast Asia, India, and North and South America.

RUBY ZOISITE

The crystal combination of ruby in zoisite is also known as anyolite. When the ruby crystals are embedded in the zoisite mineral, you have a blended-energy crystal that works through the **ROOT, HEART, AND THIRD-EYE CHAKRAS**.

This combination strengthens the flow of energy from the base chakra upward, clearing the etheric meridians of debris and repairing tears in the auric field when used in cleansings and healings. It has a stabilizing effect on the emotions, helping focus and ground them in a more rational manner. It can help clear the body of sluggish, depressive feelings by renewing a zest for life and love. It also has a harmonizing effect that balances you when you are torn between choices in your love life. It will bring the inner truth of matters to the fore, things you may already know but were afraid to see or accept. Once facing the reality of a situation, you are more likely to make a better choice for yourself, finding the inner strength to do what is best. When working with this crystal you will find that the energy of the ruby can add a little excitement to an otherwise dull outlook on life, and the zoisite can help open a more creative way of expressing yourself.

Ruby zoisite makes for a good grounding stone as well and can instill a sense of peace, having a calming effect on the spirit. Physically, it is useful for detoxification and is supportive of the main internal organs such as the heart, lungs, kidneys, liver, and bladder. On a cellular level it can help improve skin conditions. It is a good choice to aid recovery after a long illness. It has also been used to increase fertility in men and add energy and zest to spice up the sex life.

A calcium aluminum silicate mineral, it's found mostly in Brazil, India, and Tanzania.

SAPPHIRE

Blue sapphire works through
the **THROAT AND THIRD-EYE
CHAKRAS** when used in healings.

T hink of this deep-blue variety of corundum as the flip side of its sister crystal, the ruby. Both are from the same family of crystals, yet their color changes their vibratory frequency. As with other blue stones, it is a good choice to use when you are wanting to increase your psychic abilities or talents. In meditation it helps open the third eye, so a person can attune their mental and spiritual selves to a higher vibratory rate. This in turn allows them access to more of the universal truths. It's considered a good stone to pray with, elevating the subconscious mind and helping it in reaching out to connect with the angelic realms and the Divine Spirit. Sapphire is also good at adding a calming serenity to the psyche that allows you to reach deeper states of meditation. It is also a useful crystal to carry or wear as an aid in building self-esteem by bringing to light your subconscious fears and beliefs and releasing them. This act also helps increase your inner wisdom and knowledge.

As with other blue crystals, its naturally cooling nature works well to suppress inflammatory conditions. It can assist in balancing the glandular functions of the body and is a good choice for helping to diminish headaches, earaches, and vertigo, as well as helping to calm a sore throat. Place one over your forehead when you are fighting the flu, to reduce fever. Sapphire is also used in healing layouts or as an elixir for vision problems. It is recommended for those with emotional or nervous disorders, helping reduce the anxiety and stress that feed their syndromes.

Sapphire is an aluminum oxide mineral, a variety of corundum that can be found around the world, from the US to Madagascar and India to Australia.

SCOLECITE

This lovely white
stone is tranquility in
mineral form.

As a higher-vibrational crystal, it's considered a stone of peace. You can feel scolecite's calming frequency by simply holding it in your palm. It's a great choice for those who experience panic attacks or mysterious chest pains due to stress. Many people instantly experience the easing of tension in their muscles, that subtle sign that carries with it a feeling of relief. For this reason, it is a great stone to sleep with at night, as its soothing vibrations flow into your auric field, damping down any nervous energy or leftover daytime tensions. Personally, I find comfort drifting off to sleep with a scolecite in my hand most nights, simply to ensure pleasant dreams and a restful night.

Working through the crown and third-eye chakras, this crystal brings a serene enlightenment to the auric field. When meditated upon, it can lift the spirit to higher elevations and realms, aiding angelic communications and communion with heavenly sources. For those who are studying or yearning to experience astral projection, scolecite is a great stone to focus upon when reaching for those out-of-body experiences.

As a stone of union, it is often used in combination with other stones to help pair their differing attributes to work together in healings. It does especially well when paired with danburite, phenacite, or apophyllite, merging their unique characteristics into a more powerful force. Physically, it helps with most brain and neurological disorders, aiding in stabilizing the neural networks to work more effectively. It also helps with normalizing serotonin levels and the circulatory system, and strengthening the immune system. Because there are potassium and calcium ions within the crystalline structure of scolecite, it is also used in healings for the bones and teeth.

A hydrated calcium aluminum silicate (zeolite) mineral, it is found mostly in Iceland and India.

SELENITE

The basic white selenite crystal pictured works through the **THIRD-EYE, CROWN, AND STAR CHAKRAS**, located above the head, and is often used in building meditation grids.

These striated, white crystals come in different forms. Typically sold as opaque white sticklike pieces, or small towers with an otherworldly appearance, this mineral also comes in the form of a petallike flower known as the desert rose. By laying out pieces of selenite around you, then sitting or lying down inside this crystal grid, you can experience a profound effect on your meditations or healings. This surrounding energy brings about an easier attunement with the higher realms and the divine energy of the universe that can raise your own vibratory frequency. The power of these crystals helps elevate your mind to a higher dimension, while clearing blockages and cleansing the spirit. This opens a pathway for the Universal Light to enter and aid the body in returning to a normal state of health.

Since selenite is more effective on the energy fields of the body, it can easily aid the nervous system and the brain. It can be effective opening the third eye, increasing your psychic awareness and inner *knowing* of the causes of your disorders in general, thereby assisting in finding solutions to various health problems. Selenite is also a stone that can add a sense of peace and tranquility to an area. Placing one on your desk or by your bed will help keep stressful feelings and thoughts at bay.

Physically, it's used to promote spinal realignment by placing or rubbing a selenite wand along the spine to increase flexibility and movement. It is also used to work synergistically with other stones in general healing work.

Selenite is a hydrous calcium sulfate mineral normally mined in North America, Russia, Greece, and Europe. It's also found in its various forms around the world.

SEPTARIAN

Also known as dragon's-egg
stones, yellow and brown
septarian crystals are good
grounding stones and can be
USED ON ALL THE CHAKRAS.

H owever, they are especially favored for promoting self-confidence through the solar plexus and sacral chakras. They give you an extra injection of courage when facing opposing views or adversaries at work or in social situations. Septarian helps you stand your ground while giving you the strength to present your opinions in a concise and reasonable manner. And when things aren't going your way, they help you become more tolerant and patient with those you find annoying. They are also considered protective stones that work to shield your physical and astral bodies from harmful or damaging energies coming from others.

These stones are good tools for use in group projects or get-togethers as they help bring a harmony to groups of people so they can work together to accomplish a goal. This works better if everyone carries a stone, but if not, lay a few around the area in which the group is gathered to help harmonize the separate energies of everyone. The blended energies of the stone itself will go to work forming a cohesive whole that can function in unity. Another trait of septarian is that it also helps you connect with Mother Earth and tune into the natural world. It's a good choice to carry when gardening or even hiking in the woods. There's a serenity of spirit that comes when you can meditate outside in the natural world that is both cleansing and refreshing.

Septarian is a general healing stone that helps the body heal itself, and it is often used to help alleviate muscle spasms and problems with the skeletal/muscular foundations of the body.

These oddly patterned stones are a mixture of different minerals, mainly calcite, aragonite, and limestone. Deposits of septarian are found in North America, Europe, Australia, and Madagascar.

SERPENTINE

The olive-green color and markings
on this stone are the reason for
its name, because its look was
associated with the skin of snakes.

T hough it may appear in many different shades from dark to light, serpentine is primarily used to link the heart and solar plexus chakras in healing layouts. This crystal, however, is often used on the entire meridian and chakra systems when doing clearings or purifications. Serpentine is a great stone for meditations because it can awaken the higher brain functions to expand your horizons and open your mind to an understanding of the spiritual side of life. It's used in chakra cleansings to help raise the kundalini energy at the base of the spine, often pictured as a coiled cobra, on its journey through the body to the crown chakra for enlightenment. Emotionally, it helps you release the fear of change, which can be a factor in every life. It helps you embrace the transformations that are occurring in, and possibly disrupting, your normal life habits and patterns. Serpentine is a good stone to carry as it instills a sense of stability and confidence, helping to ground you amid social or personal changes. Historically, serpentine was worn as an amulet to protect against snakes, spiders, and other venomous creatures.

A good cleansing and detoxifying stone for the body, it helps clear blocked energies and allows for the natural flow of chi to be reestablished along the meridian system. It has a more metaphysical power that can help you in meditations to tap into the Akashic Records for guidance and knowledge. On a physical level, it has been used to treat constipation, IBS, parasites, and other digestive-tract issues, as well as to help combat chronic fatigue syndrome.

The green form of this magnesium silicate mineral can be found in North and South America, England, and South Africa.

SHIVA LINGHAMS

Shiva linghams are special stones
that represent the balance of
opposites, as the yin and yang.

They can be used on all the chakra centers for balancing and clearing. Shivas are most renowned for their high-energy frequency, which resonates well with those who practice daily meditation. They are powerful stones to work with when attempting to elevate your inner spirit to grow into that supreme union with the divine. They are often used to help raise the kundalini force from the base of the spine up through the chakra centers, elevating the spirit. Considered a sacred stone to Hindus, they were named after the god Shiva and are honored as a representation of his phallus and his physical union with his consort, the goddess Kali. Their egg shape is also felt to be symbolic for the creation of the universe. Some stones are naturally formed, but most are hand-shaped by area workers.

Shiva linghams have influence over the reproductive parts of our bodies and are used in healings to stabilize and encourage harmony within the hormonal glands, which allows these physical organs to function properly. Physically, they help with fertility problems and prostate troubles with men. For women they can help alleviate the miseries of menopause. Their brown coloring strengthens their link with the lower chakras, so they can aid you with lower-body backaches and pains.

Shiva linghams were traditionally taken from the river beds of the Narmada River during the drought season, where they were gathered by locals, polished, and sold. Recently it has been hard to harvest them in this manner, and so much of what is on the market today is now being mined nearby. They are a form of cryptocrystalline quartz filled with impurities over the ages that give them their brown color and markings.

Shiva linghams are from the area near the sacred Narmada River in India.

SHUNGITE

This mysterious and special black
stone comes from northwestern Russia.
Though it would normally associate
with the **ROOT CHAKRA**, its higher
**FREQUENCY LINKS IT WITH ALL THE
CHAKRA CENTERS**.

It builds confidence and gives courage, allowing you to take the lead in stressful situations and solve the problem at hand. This self-assurance can be used to manifest into reality the ideas and desires you have. It gives you stamina to help attain your goals in life, while truly teaching that if at first you don't succeed, try, try again. Success eventually comes to those who can remain calm in the face of adversity and keep going until they reach their goals.

When carried on a regular basis, tiger iron will add strength to the auric field, fortifying it against negative or harmful intrusions or attachments. This makes it a good choice to wear as a stone of protection. It helps you fight your inner fears, instilling the nerve needed to face your foes and ultimately triumph. It's a great choice of crystal to use when wanting to cleanse the lower chakras of clogs or attachments, rebalancing and aligning them to support the upper energy centers to allow for a clear flow of chi.

Physically, tiger iron is used to increase strength when exercising or training, helping tone muscles and support the skeletal structure. It's also useful for the kidneys, pancreas, and colon health, as well as helping regulate hormonal issues related to the sex organs. Tiger iron can be used during labor to help mitigate the pain as it gives the body an extra boost of vitality and strength to ward off the energy drain of childbirth.

Tiger iron is a silicon dioxide mineral banded with red jasper and hematite that is usually found in the US, India, Australia, and South Africa.

TOURMALINE

Tourmaline is most notable as a protection stone for its ability to clear the auric field of harmful and negative energies, while it purifies and strengthens the auric shield.

It's my favorite, and I always keep a piece in my car to protect against accidents. And there's also one at our register in the shop just to keep away thieves and negative people. Many of our ghost-hunting customers carry it for protection from spirit attachments and attacks.

It's great to carry at work when the surrounding environment is stressful or emotionally draining. It eases the anxiety and tensions in the surrounding atmosphere by keeping those damaging energies from entering your personal space. Linked with the root chakra, tourmaline is a very effective grounding stone that keeps you centered and focused on the work at hand. It helps stabilize your spirit and balance your emotions, so you can successfully accomplish your daily task. Place one between yourself and your computer or other electronic equipment to block the electromagnetic rays from slipping into your auric field as well as clearing the ether surrounding you. Meditating with black tourmaline can help you focus more intently as it shields your spirit from unwanted intrusions of negativity.

Sleeping with this crystal clears the aura, allowing for a restful and refreshing night's slumber as well as chasing away bad dreams that have plagued you in the past. It simply gives off a feeling of comfort and security. Physically, it can help align the spinal column when used in healing rituals and raise the energy flow from the root to the crown chakra. It has also been used to fortify the natural immune system and help the body with the elimination of toxins.

This iron aluminum boron silicate, also known as schorl, can be found in parts of North and South America, China, India, and Russia.

TURQUOISE

Certain Native American tribes
believe turquoise to be a stone of the
spirit and sky. It can be used to assist
in contacting the Divine Source.

T rue turquoise is growing harder to get and more expensive no matter what country it's from. A lot of what is currently on the market at cheaper pricing is dyed howlite or turquite, which is essentially reconstituted turquoise, and African turquoise, which is a form of jasper with similar healing associations that is mined in Africa. All are linked to the throat and heart chakras, depending on whether its color is more blue or green.

Turquoise also helps you face fear and releases the mental blocks and self-debilitating thoughts that hold you back in life. It has a calming aspect that quells the fires of rage and leads to a more detached view of what has angered you. It also facilitates communication, so problems can be talked out rather than fought out. During the early Middle Ages and before, it was often used by soldiers in the Ottoman Empire to protect themselves and was believed to give them the dispassion needed to slay their enemies without regret.

Today, we direct the energies within this stone to expand our vital forces, supporting a stronger ego that can protect itself against the slings and arrows of modern-day life. It's protective in nature and can be used to boost the energy of the auric field during meditations and when worn daily. Turquoise works to quell inflammatory conditions such as arthritis, rheumatism, and gout. It helps with the regeneration of tissue, supports oxygenation of the blood, and is used in healings for heart and lung issues affecting the breath, as well as chest colds and bronchitis. Some find it useful for muscular pain relief.

A copper aluminum phosphate mineral, true turquoise can be found in North America, Russia, China, and areas of the Middle East.

VESUVIANITE

Vesuvianite can clear out the negative vibrations and the dross accumulations in the auric field located in the middle areas of your body when used in aura cleansings. This helps strengthen your resolve on issues facing you.

This crystal was first discovered near Mt. Vesuvius in Italy back in the early 1700s. Though it is found in other colors, we will focus on the yellow-green variety pictured above, which links to the heart and solar plexus chakras. Working up through the solar plexus to the heart chakra, this crystal will link your gut feelings about circumstances in your emotional heart and encourage compassion and understanding of others in situations confronting you. It can bring courage to the individual who carries it, prompting them to stand up for what is right in the face of opposition. In meditations, it helps those who are trying to release fears and problems from past lives that have carried over into this one. It assists you in breaking patterns of negative thoughts and allows you to relax and learn to love and accept yourself for who you really are. This can help reduce those subconscious reasons for anxiety and stress that can be the reason you feel short tempered and tend to snap at those who are closest to you.

Vesuvianite works well when used in healing rituals or meditations with issues related to the heart, lungs, stomach area, and digestive processes, which makes it a good choice to carry when dieting as it fortifies your willpower and helps stabilize your metabolism. A general healing stone, its cooling nature can be used to relieve the inflammation of varicose veins and skin infections.

Vesuvianite is a calcium magnesium iron aluminum silicate hydroxide mineral. Originally discovered in Italy, it is now found in other locations, such as Canada, the US, Tanzania, and parts of Europe.

SUGGESTED CRYSTALS AND STONES BY PROBLEM OR AILMENT

Rather than present a listing of ailments and associating them with specific stones or crystals as most other books do, I prefer to set up a guidance chart that can lead you to choosing the crystal or stone that might be right for you. I will also provide a chart that specifies the other reasons people carry or wear the crystals and stones. As I stated in the beginning of this book, each type of stone or crystal carries its own unique rhythm, as does every individual person. This means that simply because amazonite works miracles for me with nerve pain in my wrist and arm, it doesn't mean that it will work miracles for you. So, rather than doing a comprehensive list of specific ailments, I will simply chart out the areas of the human body and relate these to a crystal grouping by color, as a guide for the suggested group in which to look for a suitable crystal or stone. We all are different and we all will react differently to the healing vibrations of the crystals. Yes, there are some that are well known for their general assistance with certain disorders—say, amethyst for headaches—that have been used traditionally for years and with great success for most people. However, as happy as most people are with using an amethyst for headaches, personally, they do not work for me. I've tried them three different times, laying them over my forehead, holding them to my temples, and placing them under my pillow to no avail. However, scolocite, for whatever reason, does help me. I do not suffer from headaches in general, but when I do it is mostly from stress, and scolocite simply relaxes me enough to make the headache dissipate.

That is the reason I don't necessarily go for listing ailments to disorders. I think it's wiser to trace your ailment or disorder to the part of your body it emanates from, and then choose a crystal from the associated chakra color group. Starting at this point, you can choose the crystal or stone that draws your attention and try it. If your first choice does not work, don't give up. Simply try another one and see what it does. Normally you will find the right crystal for your problem soon enough. And sometimes, you luck out, and it is the very first crystal you pick!

In the chart that follows, the first column will show the body area your problem is coming from or connected to. The next column will list the crystal color, and the final column will offer suggested crystals to start with. Essentially, look at the crystals and stones found in this grouping and see which one feels right or simply attracts you. Then start with one of these choices. If none of them call to you, then go back to the color suggested and find a crystal or stone on your own that has that color. It *doesn't have to be from the list on the right*. These are merely suggestions I offer as a good place to start your search. Always remember, it's about which crystal or stone is in harmony with you, not your friends or your relatives, or even my suggestions, but *you*. Choose a stone, carry it with you, wear it, sleep with it, and see if it helps. If you get nothing from it, then try another. There are many reasons for a lot of the disorders and ailments we suffer from, and so it only makes sense that various crystals will work differently for everyone.

For example, let's say you suffer from insomnia. Since this is generally associated with your brain, and your brain is located in your head, then you will start by looking at the Body Area column. Underneath that listing you will find the crown and third-eye chakras linked to that body part. So, you would start your search from the white, clear, and purple color groups of crystals and stones. Some of the recommended ones are amethyst, calcite, jade, scolocite, etc. After choosing the one you like best, sleep with it to see if it helps. Your insomnia might be caused from an overactive mindset, one that won't turn off at night. You simply have too many ideas racing around that keep you awake. Or, it could be you are worried or frustrated over an incident that happened, and you can't stop replaying the scene in your mind, trying to rectify or change the outcome. And, of course, it could be that you have restless-leg syndrome and tend to toss and turn and kick, and that physical restlessness is what is keeping you from a good night's sleep. All three reasons are different and might call for three different stones. The restless mind and mental worrying generally have their foundation in the brain; therefore, the white and purple crystals should work well to calm that overactive mind. However, the physical restlessness can also be caused by the neurons misfiring inside the brain. Though your legs are located at the bottom of your body, you can see how

they are affected by your neural network, causing the jerking motions. In this instance, if the white or purple stones do not work, you might try a blue or green stone for its cooling and calming effect on your overall nervous system.

The next time you go to a crystal shop, walk around, pick up and hold the stones in the appropriate color groups, and, if it feels right, purchase it. Try it out for a few nights and see if it helps. If not, then go and choose a different one that you think might help. Working with the crystals is a trial-and-error type of situation. And though that may not be what you want to hear, I believe it to be the truth. What's good for the goose is simply not always good for the gander, something I have learned in my years of selling crystals and stones. However, I find that most people will intuitively pick the right stone or at least navigate to the right group of stones when they are seeking relief. It took me a few tries before I found that pink stones are the best for stress relief and calming my anxieties, while white stones, particularly scolecite, help me sleep soundly with sweet dreams. Black tourmaline is my go-to for protection, and green stones, such as aventurine, seem to keep prosperity knocking at my door as far as business is concerned. I'm still waiting to hit the lottery but am content knowing the bills are paid and there's always enough to go around for life's little pleasures! I tend to believe in keeping things simple and, therefore, hope the chart that follows can help find the right stone for you!

CRYSTAL REFERENCE CHARTS

Crystal Healing Chart

BODY AREA / CHAKRA	CRYSTAL COLOR	CRYSTAL SUGGESTIONS
head: crown & third-eye chakras	clear, purple, white	amethyst, calcite, howlite, quartz, scolocite, selenite, white jade
neck: throat chakra	blue	angelite, blue lace agate, blue aragonite, lapis lazuli, sodalite
heart: heart chakra	green, pink	aventurine, chrysocolla, malachite, rose quartz, rhodochrosite
stomach: sacral chakra	gold, yellow	yellow calcite, citrine, yellow jaspers, moonstone, tiger eye
abdomen: solar plexus chakra	brown, gold, orange	brown aragonite, carnelian, goldstone, sunstone, tiger eye
lower body/spine: root chakra	red, black	astrophyllite, garnet, red jasper, obsidian, ruby, black tourmaline

Other Crystal Uses

REASON	CRYSTAL COLOR	CRYSTAL SUGGESTIONS
abundance, prosperity	green	aventurine, chrysocolla, moss agate, peridot
business, success	orange, gold, green	aventurine, carnelian, goldstone, tiger iron
courage	red, orange	carnelian, garnet, red jasper, ruby
creativity	clear, blue, purple	lapis lazuli, lepidolite, quartz, sodalite
fear releasing	red, orange, gold	carnelian, red jaspers, tiger eye
general healing	all	aragonite, mookaite jasper, quartz, selenite, shungite
grief	pink, white	rose quartz, selenite, rhodochrosite
grounding	black, brown, red	red jasper, obsidian, onyx, shungite, tiger eye, tiger iron, tourmaline
happiness, joy	yellow, orange, white	amber, citrine, sunstone, scolecite, yellow calcite
love	pink, green	aventurine, chrysocolla, peridot, ruby, rose quartz, pink opal
mental focus	black, blue, brown, purple	lepidolite, lapis lazuli, tiger eye, shungite
nature connections	green	aventurine, moss agate, tree agate
protection	black, purple	amethyst, jet, hematite, onyx, obsidian, shungite, black tourmaline
psychic empowerment	purple, clear, blue, black	amethyst, astrophyllite, labradorite, lepidolite, onyx, obsidian, quartz, rainbow moonstone, shungite
stress relief	blue, pink, white	blue lace agate, celestite, moonstone, pink opal, clear quartz, rose quartz, selenite, turquoise

Crystal Groups Index

Crystal Index

BIBLIOGRAPHY

Campbell, Dan. *Edgar Cayce on the Power of Color, Stones, and Crystals*. Edited by Charles Thomas Cayce. New York: Warner Books, 1989.

Cunningham, Scott. *Cunningham's Encyclopedia of Crystal, Gem & Metal Magic*. 11th ed. Woodbury, MN: Llewellyn, 2012.

De Long, Douglas. *Ancient Healing Techniques: A Course in Psychic & Spiritual Development*. St. Paul, MN: Llewellyn, 2012.

Gienger, Michael. *Healing Crystals: The A–Z Guide to 430 Gemstones*. Translated by Chinwendu Uzodike. Forres, Scotland: Earthdancer, 2009.

Hall, Judy. *The Crystal Bible: A Definitive Guide to Crystals*. Cincinnati, OH: Walking Stick, 2003.

Hawking, Stephen. *The Universe in a Nutshell*. New York: Random House, 2005.

Healing Crystals. www.healingcrystals.com. Accessed August 10, 2018.

Lilly, Sue, and Simon Lilly. *Healing with Crystals and Chakra Energies: How to Harness the Transforming Power of Colour, Crystals and Your Body's Own Subtle Energies to Increase Health and Wellbeing*. London: Hermes House, 2011.

Simmons, Robert. *The Pocket Book of Stones: Who They Are & What They Teach*. Berkeley, CA, North Atlantic Books, 2015.

Yogananda. *Autobiography of a Yogi: 60th Anniversary Edition*. Self-Realization Fellowship, 1993.

Zukav, Gary. *The Dancing Wu Li Masters: An Overview of the New Physics*. New York: HarperOne, 2009.

ABOUT THE AUTHOR

Kate O'Dell's interest in crystals began in the 1970s, when she purchased her first crystal book and her first quartz crystal. After leaving her career as a professional seamstress behind, she followed her true desire and in 2010 opened The Crystal Wand in Gettysburg, Pennsylvania. To help her customers know what they were purchasing, she began writing brief descriptions of all the stones and gave them out with each one sold. Her accumulated knowledge of the crystals and stones comes from her own in-depth research and stories shared with everyday customers who came through the shop. She lives in Gettysburg with two cats and a house full of crystals and stones.